The Rediscovery of
Apocalyptic

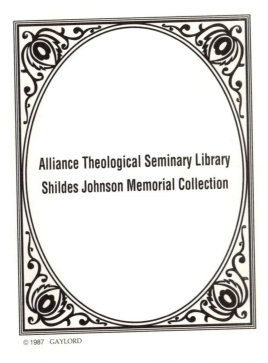

STUDIES IN BIBLICAL THEOLOGY

Second Series · 22

THE REDISCOVERY OF APOCALYPTIC

*A polemical work on a neglected
area of biblical studies and its
damaging effects on theology and
philosophy*

KLAUS KOCH

SCM PRESS LTD
BLOOMSBURY STREET LONDON

Translated by Margaret Kohl from the German
Ratlos ver der Apokalyptik
(Gütersloher Verlagshaus Gerd Mohn, Gütersloh 1970)

334 013615

First British edition 1972
published by SCM Press Ltd
56 Bloomsbury Street London

© SCM Press Ltd 1972

Computerised origination by Autoset, Brentwood

PRINTED IN GREAT BRITAIN
BY W & J MACKAY LIMITED, CHATHAM

CONTENTS

ABBREVIATIONS

BevTh	Beiträge zur evangelischen Theologie
BZNW	Beiheft zur *Zeitschrift für die neutestament-liche Wissenschaft*
ET	English translation
EvTh	*Evangelische Theologie*
ExpT	*Expository Times*
FRLANT	Forschungen zur Religion und Literatur des Alten und Neuen Testaments
GCS	Die griechischen christlichen Schriftsteller der ersten Jahrhunderts
HNT	Handbuch zum Neuen Testament
HZ	*Historische Zeitschrift*
JBL	*Journal of Biblical Literature*
KuD	*Kerygma und Dogma*
NF	Neue Folge (=new series)
NovT	*Novum Testamentum*
RGG	*Die Religion in Geschichte und Gegenwart*
TDNT	*Theological Dictionary of the New Testament* (ET of *TWNT*)
ThB	Theologische Bücherei
TLZ	*Theologische Literaturzeitung*
TR	*Theologische Rundschau*
TWNT	*Theologisches Wörterbuch zum Neuen Testament*
WMANT	Wissenschaftliche Monographien zum Alten und Neuen Testament
WUNT	Wissenschaftliche Untersuchungen zum Neuen Testament
ZAW	*Zeitschrift für die alttestamentliche Wissenschaft*
ZNW	*Zeitschrift für die neutestamentliche Wissenschaft*
ZTK	*Zeitschrift für Theologie und Kirche*

I

THE PURPOSE OF THIS BOOK

The historical and critical investigation of the biblical writings is viewed at the present time with growing dissatisfaction, both within the theological world and outside it. At the end of the nineteenth century theological liberalism felt historical exegesis to be a glorious liberation from hide-bound dogmatism, and German scholars supported it with pride in its irreproachable methods and scientific objectivity. Today it is being pushed aside by many students of theology and clergy as being remote from present reality and hence unproductive - a theory with no access to practice. In the last century and at the beginning of our own there were certainly people who, for reasons of faith, held historical research in the biblical sphere to be inadmissible. These fundamentalist voices can still be heard today, without their seriously influencing orthodox theology. What is new about the present situation, however, is that it is the very theologians who claim to be 'progressive' who are particularly vocal in their disparagement of historical exegesis; they feel that historical theology has done its work and achieved all the results open to it, and that it is accordingly time for us to pass on to other, more modern themes - sociology and psychology, for example. This is not the place to enter either into fundamentalist disputations or into revolutionary programmes. In what follows it is my intention merely to single out one small, not unimportant sector, in order to flood-light the question of whether historical-critical theology has now performed its function.

Has biblical scholarship really done everything that it was possible to do by historical methods? We need only pick out one point in order to be disconcerted by the answer: the historical role of the person of Jesus. Seldom has there been such a spectrum of different interpretations of the historical Jesus as there is in present-day scholarship. If information on this head was necessary, it was provided by the press and radio reports on the German Evangelical Church conference which took place in Stuttgart in July 1969 and over its working group on 'The Jesus Controversy'. The multiplicity of mutually contradictory hypotheses on this subject - a subject so truly basic to the whole of Christianity from its very beginnings - may partly result from the fragmentary and imperfect nature of the historical sources, in this case of the synoptic gospels particularly. But is it not also due to the way in which the exegetes chase busily along well-worn paths after problems of philological detail, without sufficiently having an eye for the total historical context? In spite of all the exhaustive hermeneutical discussion (though this has admittedly diminished in recent years), is the exegete's historical consciousness perhaps undeveloped, even though he is working along historical lines? As we all know, historical and critical exegesis means explaining a biblical text against the background of the circumstances existing at the time, i.e., on the basis of the conditions and potentialities of its temporal, geographical and linguistic environment. But if this is so, then genuine historical work is only being done where the texts are illuminated by the complete political, economic, religious and linguistic sweep of the biblical world. The genesis of the biblical statements only really assumes concrete historical form against this background. Can the widespread uncertainty about the historical Jesus - more, the common difficulty of finding a generally convincing way of access to the present from the biblical writings of the past - perhaps be explained by the fact that New Testament scholarship (and in its way Old Testament scholarship as well) has failed to think consistently historically, confining itself to minutiae and dispensing with real historical clarity? Perhaps the motive is to avoid the suspicion of reconstruction and speculation. Perhaps, too, the aim is to pass quickly from the attendant historical circumstances to a kerygma which is supposedly of equally paramount importance for all ages alike.

In the following pages we shall not be concerning ourselves with an account of research into the person of Jesus, let alone with the state of exegetical scholarship in general. We shall turn our attention to a relatively small area, one which lies on the fringe of the canon but which is bound to be considered whenever the point at issue is the historical close of the Old Testament and the historical circumstances surrounding the rise of Jesus of Nazareth. How far this area, which is documented by the apocalyptic writings, reflects a legitimate final stage in the religion of the Old Testament and how far it plays a determining part for the origins of Jesus and primitive Christianity may remain undecided. It is sufficient for our purpose to note that one group of theologians maintains that apocalyptic possesses a significance of this kind for the end of the Old Testament and the beginning of the New, whereas another group denies it with equal pertinacity. Since the two parties at least agree that a 'yes' or 'no' in this dispute makes an essential difference to one's view of the historical and theological transition from Israel to early Christianity, there is no need for me to set up a new theory about what the actual relationship is. I shall therefore confine myself to bringing out *how* the different theologians arrive at their 'yes' or 'no'. Apocalyptic serves as a touchstone for the extent to which exegetes work consistently historically, i.e., how far they really transpose themselves into the spirit of the age which they profess to be talking about. (In addition, apocalyptic fascinates those theologians and philosophers who concern themselves with the future aspects of human society. But, as we shall see, this group of problems is always associated with the internal biblical ones to which I have just referred wherever people have recourse to the apocalyptic outlook. For that reason we do not need to go into it here.)

The conclusion of our present investigation is that a deeper historical consciousness is only seldom to be found among the exegetes when they are dealing with apocalyptic, either positively or negatively. More, even the critical historical methods which have been familiar for decades are only inadequately applied to this field. Instead, particular stereotypes and prejudices are carried over from decade to decade. Even the relatively narrow field of apocalyptic shows why contemporary theology gives such excessively imprecise answers to so many questions affecting the Old and New Testaments. Anyone who follows up the contradictory opinions about apocalyptic in late Israel and early Christianity in the relevant theological and philosophical literature discovers a tender spot in present biblical scholarship and finds himself forced to the conclusion that, in spite of remarkable individual achievements, scholars are still far from an adequate overall historical grasp of their subject.

It is my firm personal belief that today theology is more necessary than ever and, moreover, that theology cannot get along in the future without reliable historical foundations. This conviction made a neutral studies report impossible. This book is intended to be controversial. Its aim is to expose the present state of affairs as untenable and to provoke its amendment, even if it is by the way of contradiction. Unfortunately it has been impossible to avoid controversy with certain of my colleagues at various points, much as I value and admire their achievements in other areas of study. But I have felt bound to show that their theories about the apocalyptic writings are inadequately supported and unfortunate in their results. Nothing would please me more than to be shown my mistake at these points through a speedy and detailed refutation of my criticisms.

II

THE APOCALYPTIC RENAISSANCE

1. About ten years ago, unexpectedly for exegetical scholarship and theology in general, the term apocalyptic re-emerged from the depths and became a hotly disputed slogan. Generally speaking, apocalyptic is understood to mean a complex of writings and ideas which were widespread about the turn of the era in Palestine, in the Israelite diaspora and in early Christian circles; but which can also appear in similar form in other religious situations and mental climates. In the previous fifty years Palestinian writings dating from the turn of the era had almost been forgotten. Apocalyptic literature had never played any part in university courses in theology. Even today it is nowhere an examination subject. Apocalyptic themes and ideas seemed to present no special problems to scholars - still less did they appear to have any significance for non-exegetical theology. Even today Kautzsch's edition of the apocrypha and pseudepigrapha (1900),[1] P. Volz's *Jüdische Eschatologie von Daniel bis Akiba* (1903)[2] and Wilhelm Bousset's *Religion des Judentums im Neutestamentlichen Zeitalter* (1902)[3] are the only standard works in German in our field. It is significant, however, that all three books have been reprinted in the last ten years.[4]

This sudden turning to apocalyptic has only to a small extent been conditioned by a fresh study of the texts. Its main, if indirect, impetus comes from the questionings of New Testament scholarship or systematic theology. This explains why the rediscovery of apocalyptic themes was immediately associated with a high theological estimate which has, understandably enough, roused opposition among other theologians and philosophers and has evoked a still stronger condemnation of historical apocalyptic among opponents of the trend.

For a wide theological public, at least in Germany and Switzerland, apocalyptic was rescued from its obscure status as an odd, specialist field in the history of religion by Ernst Käsemann's essay on 'The Beginnings of Christian Theology', published in 1960.[5] His investigation finds its climax in a sentence which has given rise to much discussion since: 'Apocalyptic was the mother of all Christian theology - since we cannot really class the preaching of Jesus as theology.' Here apocalyptic is understood as the legitimate continuation of Old Testament ideas and therefore as the link which joins the Old Testament and the New. Although Käsemann's thesis had its forerunners and although other exegetes besides supported similar ideas, it was Käsemann's exposition which first roused attention, and indeed excitement. For one thing, in the sentence just quoted Käsemann put the problem in more radical form than any other writer had done; for another, such a standpoint was least of all expected from a pupil of the famous New Testament scholar Bultmann. Other of Bultmann's followers were just as shocked by this as conservative scholars. Up to then apocalyptic had been for biblical scholarship something on the periphery of the Old and New Testaments - something bordering on heresy. Käsemann had suddenly declared that a tributary was the main stream, from which everything else at the end of the Old Testament and the beginning of the New was allegedly fed.

In the systematic field, Wolfhart Pannenberg had a year previously already reintroduced the apocalyptic concept of history, maintaining that it was both the presupposition of the historical thinking of the west and the horizon which spans the whole of Christian theology in general.[6] Since these were the notions of a systematic theologian (and moreover one who was then still unknown), Pannenberg did not at first rouse the same opposition as Käsemann. In actual fact, however, Pannenberg's acceptance of apocalyptic ideas meant a much more thorough overturning of the centre of current theological consciousness than was the case with Käsemann. But we shall be considering this point at a later stage. What Käsemann and Pannenberg engendered in certain of the younger German theologians may be called a positive apocalyptic renaissance.

The apocalyptic renaissance is in any case a remarkable event in the history of biblical interpretation. One sector of Holy Scripture seems to be pushing itself into the foreground and to be claiming a special status for itself in theological studies. It has occasionally been known, in the history of the church, for the Pauline corpus, the Johannine writings, or the prophets to provide guide-lines for the whole theological system. But for a collection of writings on the border-line between canon and apocrypha to acquire this status is unique, at least in academic theology. The apocalyptic writings in the selection offered by the canon of the Protestant churches (largely, that is to say, limited to Revelation and the book of Daniel) were for centuries solely the arena of sects, which were looked down upon by academic theology with contempuous superiority. If apocalyptic literature is suddenly beginning to play a dominant role in theology itself, there must be reasons for it; and we must try to discover what these are. Moreover we still have to enquire whether it is really historical apocalyptic which is looming up so suddenly at the centre of theological thinking. There is a widespread suspicion that, basically, certain contemporary ideas are being projected back and fathered upon the apocalyptic writers; whether the reason be to make modern ideas more cogent and plausible, or whether it be to represent certain contemporary theological ideas as being from the outset unbiblical and uncanonical. The apocalyptic writings could be particularly suited to such conscious or unconscious manipulation, because little work has been done on them by scholars and they have always for that reason appeared to observers as equivocal and open to many interpretations.

This book is a contribution to a controversy and as such attaches no importance to comprehensiveness; I have simply picked up whatever has been of influence. At the same time I have stressed the bearing of hypotheses about apocalyptic literature on our present general theological and mental situation, in which discussion about apocalyptic has taken on a particular acrimony. Developments in Germany have stood relatively on their own and independent of international research (which is by no means necessarily an advantage).

I have devoted a special chapter to the research of English-speaking scholars, although I have not tried to classify it within the history of thought and theology - a difficult task from a continental standpoint. French literature has contributed surprisingly little to our subject; consequently I have only touched on it briefly. (To cover all the secondary sources would be the task of years or decades and the resulting basic picture would probably be little different.)

Before marshalling argument and counter-argument, it would seem advisable to gather together some facts of literary history about apocalyptic, so as to show how vaguely and cloudily the term is used in the present debate and in order to try to find a point of departure for the following discussion. Only then can we go on to give a critical account of the discussion among Old and New Testament scholars, as well as in the fields of systematic theology and philosophy.

It is my intention to point out current positions in their relation to one another and in their mutual contrasts, inserting critical comments at points where the disparity between the theory and the individual apocalyptic texts threatens to become too great for the onlooker. These comments are anything but exhaustive. They are not an attempt to set up a new position alongside those already put forward. For that the time is not yet ripe and the state of research, as we shall see, is too unsatisfactory.

It is not my purpose, either, to give a comprehensive survey of the subject within theology and the history of thought as a whole. For this there is not yet either the temporal distance or the inner detachment which is required in the case of a theme which excites such strong feelings. For that reason I have chosen a broad division along the lines of the classical theological disciplines as well as those of philosophy. In the course of this discussion I hope to show how in each discipline the newly emerging apocalyptic question is reflected in its own appropriate modification. At the same time it is my intention to point out what difference this highly varying evaluation makes to the individual scholar; how much his picture of the rise of Christianity - even of Christianity's right to existence at all - is bound up with the apocalyptic problem.

For that reason we shall look, above all, for the particular prior understanding of apocalyptic which is involved - often unconsciously - among the historic and systematic theologians. The main angles of approach are as follows:

(a) How is apocalyptic specifically defined?
(b) What status does the apocalyptic so defined enjoy in the total historical or theological outlook of the writer in question?
(c) What earlier secondary literature has determined his viewpoint and assessment?
(d) Are there any signs that the writer has concerned himself with the primary texts?

I am presupposing that every sincere commentator is convinced that historical results can be, and ought to be, of relevance to systematic theology and philosophy. It is therefore completely conceivable - and why should it not also be desirable? - that apocalyptic research may also provide stimuli for the theology and philosophy of our time. But if this is to be so, it is essential for it to penetrate to the sources and to fit them into a total historical context. If that is the starting point, prejudices which have become current coin are bound to disappear of themselves. Eager appeals to the present status of apocalyptic, and equally eager denials of that status, seem to stand in danger of no longer being historical in this sense. That is why this book was written.

Historical research can certainly never get along without preliminary ideas and conceded premises. But it ceases to be research once these preliminary ideas harden into prejudices. If we are not to fall victims to the same fault of which we are accusing others, we must first ask what apocalyptic can usefully be taken to mean. What is apocalyptic?

III

WHAT IS APOCALYPTIC? AN ATTEMPT AT A PRELIMINARY DEFINITION

1. The cloudiness of current definitions

Apocalyptic is a Greek borrowing and smacks not only of the weird and menacing; it also suggests the abstruse and fantastic.[1] Since it is in its very origin a word derived from biblical scholarship, this meaning can only be explained by the fact that in the last century apocalyptic increasingly became for theologians 'the quintessence of what is "eschatologically" improper'. 'Theological eschatology believed that it could best prove its legitimacy by abjuring apocalyptic as firmly and vocally as possible.'[2] It is customary 'to term "apocalyptic" those descriptions of the future which serve as pure speculations merely to satisfy human curiosity, without any actual interest in salvation.'[3]

Christians and Jews[4] are largely speaking at one in this rejection. It is astonishing, however, that the German translation of the original Greek noun *apokalypsis, Offenbarung,* or revelation, is high up on the list of 'positive' theological terms. How can this discrepancy between the original word and its translation be explained?

The adjective apocalyptic is not directly derived from the general theological term *apokalypsis,* in the sense of revelation, at all; it comes from a second and narrower use of the word, also documented in the ancient church, as the title of literary compositions which resemble the book of Revelation,[5] i.e., secret divine disclosures about the end of the world and the heavenly state. The word apocalypse has become the usual term for this type of book. It is also applied to books and parts of books to which the ancient church did not as yet give this title - for example the synoptic apocalypse of Mark 13 (and its parallels). The ancient church already viewed the apocalyptic books with considerable reserve and hence excluded the apocalypses of Peter and Paul from the canon, as well as Christian apocalypses which were attributed to Old Testament figures (V and VI Ezra, for example).

Many early Christian apocalypses have as a result disappeared for ever, or have only recently been rediscovered - the Greek version of the apocalypse of Peter, for example, or the apocalyptic writings from the great Nag-Hammadi discoveries.[6]

In the last two hundred years historical scholarship has gone over to the practice of classifying Old Testament books and parts of books also as apocalypses, whenever (like the New Testament Book of Revelation) they contain visions of the events of the end-time and catechetical matter associated with these things. Many Old Testament scholars would assign Isa. 24-27 (the Isaiah Apocalypse), Trito-Zechariah (Zech. 12-14) and the book of Joel to this category; and all of them would include the book of Daniel and the apocryphal IV Ezra or Ezra Apocalypse. Nineteenth-century discoveries swelled the group of such writings in the Old Testament field more than in the New. In 1800 Sayce published I Enoch (Ethiopian Enoch), which had been brought back to England by an African traveller. In 1866 Ceriani brought out his edition of II Baruch (or the Syriac Apocalypse of Baruch), which he had found in an Italian library. It was followed in 1897 by Bonwetsch's edition of the Apocalypse of Abraham, based on a Slavonic manuscript. The series continued, down to the discovery after the Second World War of the numerous Qumran texts in the caves of the Dead Sea area, among which there is considerable apocalyptic material,[7] much of it still awaiting publication.

Through the continual emergence of new writings, the centre of gravity of apocalyptic literature is increasingly shifting for the historical observer from the New Testament to the Old Testament field. The number of late Israelite apocalypses is not only considerably greater today than the number of early Christian ones; the former are also, in the opinion of many scholars, much richer in content and show a greater depth of thought. That is why even 'introductions to the New Testament', when talking about apocalypses other than Revelation, only think of the late Israelite ones and do not consider the other Christian apocalypses worth mentioning.[8]

According to the prevailing opinion, the great mass of apocalyptic literature came into being between 200 BC and AD 100 in the world of Semitic-speaking (or at least strongly Semitically influenced) Israel and Jewish Christianity. The church rejected the apocalyptic writings, viewing them as apocryphal in proportion to the degree in which it later found its centre of gravity in the Greek-speaking world. The same process of elimination took place in the early Judaism organized by the Rabbis after AD 70; perhaps this was due to disappointment over the breakdown of high-flown eschatological hopes in the two risings against Rome.

During the last century a collective term 'apocalyptic' has come into general use, side by side with the generic name apocalypse. It is applied not only to the common mental and spiritual background of the relevant late Israelite and early Christian writings but is used to characterize a certain kind of religious speculation about the future of man and the world. The meaning of the adjective apocalyptic, which we mentioned above, is generally determined by this collective term.

Difficulties in defining the term apocalyptic more precisely, however, immediately arise once it ceases to be filled out merely speculatively, according to the subjective taste of the individual theologian or philosopher, but has also to be brought into accord with the historical texts.

The spiritual bond which unites the various writings classified as apocalypses is only difficult to establish because most of the Old Testament apocalypses are not extant in their original form but only in second-hand or even third-hand translations - translations in whose reliability scholars have but little confidence, and in which, moreover, we have to reckon with additions, omissions, etc. In the case of the early Christian apocalypses, on the other hand, there is a problem of literary criticism, which is not unanimously settled: how far are these apocalypses revisions of late Israelite originals? This is already a matter of debate for the synoptic apocalypse, Mark 13, and for the book of Revelation, and it is even more controversial for V and VI Ezra and the Testaments of the Twelve Patriarchs.

If there was really a community of ideas and spirit between the different books which we now call apocalypses, these books must go back to a common sociological starting point; they must have a comparable *Sitz im Leben*. The majority of scholars do in fact assume this to be the case with the Old Testament apocalyptic. But as soon as it is a question of pinning down this assumption in precise terms, the secondary literature shows an unsurpassed jumble of opinions. During the period between 200 BC and AD 100 - that is to say the late Israelite period - in which the mass of the apocalyptic writings came into being, Israel had an appearance of anything but unity, whether in Palestine or in the Diaspora. Even in primitive Christianity there was a lack of that dogmatic and organizational unity which was later to be the mark of the catholic churches of East and West. Consequently the classification of a group of writings which contains no express information about its sociological setting forces the observer into conjecture. Every one of the groupings of the late Israelite period for which we have any evidence at all has been suggested as the *Sitz im Leben* of the apocalyptic writings. Were the authors of these writings obscure and simple people, far removed from the Jerusalem hierarchy and its theology (the view held by Bousset among others)? Or did they, on the contrary, belong to a small class of highly learned sages, who were also thoroughly familiar with the non-Israelite culture of their time?[9] Does the predominating East Aramaic element and the prevalence of Babylonian material in the book of Daniel suggest that we must look for the beginnings in the Babylonian Diaspora or further east in Persia?[10] Or was this a native Palestinian growth (the opinion held by most scholars)? Were the writers part of the Essene movement (Hilgenfeld's view),[11] like the Qumran sect from whom the Dead Sea manuscripts derive, or did they belong to the Essenes' forerunners, the Hasidim (Ploeger), the pietists of the Maccabean period? Was the Pharisaic lay movement, with its strict adherence to the Law - a movement both familiar and notorious from the pages of the New Testament - its matrix (Charles)? Or even the Zealots, the unremitting fomenters of rebellion against the foreign domination of Rome?[12]

But perhaps the attempt to find out to which of the religious parties the apocalyptists belonged is a fruitless one; perhaps they were to be found among all parties at the time (Russell)? Our survey indicates how completely obscure the sociological basis of the apocalyptic writings still is.

We are no better off as regards the *Sitz im Leben* of the New Testament apocalypses. Most commentators consider that the synoptic apocalypse had its origin in Palestine before AD 70. More can hardly be discovered. According to its opening chapter, the book of Revelation was written on an Aegean island by a man called John, who merely describes himself as the servant of God or prophet and, on the evidence of his letters, had some kind of authority over the churches in Asia Minor. As for the noncanonical apocalypses, here scholars are completely in the dark.

Not only have scholars placed the *Sitz im Leben* of the apocalyptic writings as differently as it is possible to conceive; in addition it is a matter of doubt how far particular writings are to be classified as apocalypses at all. Does the so-called Isaiah Apocalypse (Isa. 24-27) or the Shepherd of Hermas really deserve the name of apocalypse? Even where the ancient church assigned the title apocalypse to a particular writing, this classification is only useful for a literary and historical assessment up to a point. A title of this kind not only heads writings such as II Baruch and the Apocalypse of Abraham, which certainly derive from the Semitic linguistic area; it is also applied to originally Hellenistic works such as II Enoch, IV Baruch and the Apocalypse of Paul, which certainly treat of heavenly journeys and cosmic geography, like the Semitic books, but which are lacking in an account of the end-time, as well as in paraenesis and historical surveys, which occupy large sections of the Hebrew and Aramaic apocalypses. The ancient church used the term from a different point of view from that of the modern literary historian. Since the Semitically determined apocalypses have come more and more to the fore during the last century, when scholars speak of apocalyptic today it is this group of writings of which they are primarily thinking.

2. A preliminary demonstration of the apocalypse
as a literary type

If we now enquire what can really be gathered from the
writings generally classified as apocalypses about the actual
apocalyptic content, the answers of different scholars vary just
as much as their above-mentioned attempts to fix the *Sitz im
Leben*. If, therefore, we are to have a standard of judgment for
the following survey and for our criticism of present attempts,
the only course open to us is to enumerate briefly a few facts
about the writings which form the basis of the discussion, so
that the reader may have a rough preliminary concept at his
disposal. Consequently I may perhaps be permitted to
formulate two dogmatic presuppositions, in the hope that
unprejudiced fellow-scholars will approve them as working
hypotheses.

1. If we are to arrive at a historical perception of the
background against which apocalyptic ideas grew up, as well as
a serviceable and generally applicable concept of apocalyptic,
we must start from the writings which were composed in
Hebrew or Aramaic, or in which, at least, the Hebrew or
Aramaic spirit is dominant. To this group belong first and
foremost the book of Daniel, I Enoch, II Baruch, IV Ezra, the
Apocalypse of Abraham and the book of Revelation, with its
Semitic tendencies.

2. We can only ascertain what is apocalyptic about these
writings if characteristics common to the type can be
demonstrated.[13] If we are to succeed at all in the future in
arriving at a binding definition of apocalyptic, a starting point
in form criticism and literary and linguistic history is, in the
nature of things, the only one possible.[14]

Given these assumptions, let me indicate in broad outline
what can be discovered. I make no claim to an adequate
description of apocalyptic as a historical phenomenon, much
less to an answer to the question of what apocalyptic actually
is. My aim is merely to furnish a number of aspects which at all
events belong to the apocalyptic sphere - if, indeed, it is
meaningful to use a word of this kind at all or to consider
historical factors as contributing to the formation of the
concept.

There are not a few scholars who declare that form-critical considerations are hopeless from the outset for apocalyptic material, which they find merely 'a hotch-potch of the most varied literary forms'.[15] This thesis cannot be refuted, strictly speaking, since there are as yet no form-critical investigations of the apocalyptic writings. But there are features of the texts which positively demand form-critical investigation and which, pending proof of the contrary, certainly convey the impression that there really was something like an apocalyptic type of writing. These features are as follows:

(i) As soon as one passes from the reading of the other Old Testament writings, the great *discourse cycles* leap to the eye. As a rule they extend over several chapters and record a long dialogue between the apocalyptic seer and his heavenly counterpart. These discourse cycles are frequently called 'visions',[16] although the vision can be replaced by mere audition (as is already the case in Dan.9). They reveal something about the destiny of mankind which has hitherto been a secret (*raz, mysterion*) guarded in heaven but which will soon come to pass on earth and which will be of absolutely decisive importance for everyone involved. The seer's partner is an exalted representative of the heavenly hierarchy. It is an obvious step to think of the Old Testament prophetic books as being a preliminary stage to the apocalyptic discourse cycles; for there vision and audition were already coupled from the eighth century BC onwards (Amos 7) and a dialogue takes place between the prophet and his God, which is limited in the post-exilic period to a dialogue between the prophet and an *angelus interpres* (e.g., Zechariah's 'night visions'). The apocalyptic cycle associates a whole series of formal characteristics with the account of the prophetic vision. To take only one of these: the first great vision cycle in Revelation begins like many other apocalyptic ones: 'After this I looked, and lo, in heaven an open door' (4.1). Amos begins the account of his vision very similarly: 'Thus the Lord God showed me: behold, he was forming locusts' (7.1). In both cases the word 'see' is part of the introduction. Then follows the exclamation or imperative 'lo' or 'behold' accompanied by a participle (in both the Greek and the Hebrew) which points to a supernatural state of affairs,[17] which immediately changes into movement. If the discourse cycle does not begin with a divine visionary disclosure, then attention is first drawn to a tormenting problem which harrasses the seer and even produces a bodily change in him. John, who was banished 'on account of the word of God', found himself 'in the Spirit on the Lord's day' (Rev. 1.10). Similarly, the introduction to IV Ezra says that because of the destruction of Zion Ezra's 'spirit was stirred profoundly'.

(ii) These *spiritual turmoils* are, according to the unanimous assertion of the apocalyptists, also the result of the unexpected experience of vision and audition. In view of the prospects of the future which are opened up to him the seer is overcome by fear and dismay, which he reports in formalized phraseology. The recipient is beside himself; he falls to the ground, his trance sometimes being heightened to the point of unconsciousness.[18] This can even lead to the feeling of a violently produced change of place (I Enoch 17.1; Apoc. Abraham 15).

It is hardly possible to ascertain how far descriptions of this kind are representations of an actual experience and how far they are a literary fashion - a mannered over-refinement of the prophet's account of his reception of the Word (Ezek. 2.1; 3.12-15; and frequently elsewhere). They are at least signs of a literary relationship.

(iii) The seer does not stop at the description of his own state or even at the secrets and revolutions of the future. He draws conclusions for his readers, offering them to his community, or his disciples or 'sons', in the form of *paraenetic discourses*. These sections are invariably separate from the visionary or auditory discourse cycles. They unfold a kind of eschatological ethic, which calls still-faithful members of the people of God to endurance even under persecution, because the present age of darkness will soon be at an end (cf. the letters in Revelation; the final discourse and letter in II Bar.; IV Ezra 14.27-36; the paraenetic book in I Enoch). The generic characteristics of the paraenetic sections, as well as the origins of the form, are still uninvestigated.[19] In Daniel and in the Apocalypse of Abraham the paraenetic sections are replaced by *introductory legends*, which are apparently intended to propound examples of proper behaviour. Here too the literary character is still obscure.[20] But to unite visionary - auditory discourse cycles

and paraenetic sections as component types evidently belongs
to the true apocalypse.

(iv) It is a curious fact that later Israelite and early Christian
apocalyptic writers do not reveal their names or the period in
which they are writing, but positively hide behind a man of
God belonging to the past: behind Enoch, for instance ('the
seventh generation from Adam'): or Ezra and Daniel, men of
the Exile; but also behind Peter or Paul, as the apostolic
guarantors of the founding era of the church. The book of
Revelation seems to be a unique exception. This *pseudonymity*
is a much discussed but not convincingly explained
phenomenon.[21] It is only clear formally, as being the mark of a
literary type. As such it differs from the contemporary Wisdom
pseudonymous literature (Ecclesiastes, the Wisdom of
Solomon) and its cultic counterpart (the Psalms of Solomon,
the Prayer of Manasses) by its avoidance of royal names as
literary cloak.

(v) The language takes on a concealed meaning by means of
mythical images rich in symbolism. The forces of history and of
the present, i.e., the forces of the world-time (*'olam, aion*) are
reduced to their outstanding basic characteristics, appearing as
dangerous, often unnaturally degenerate beasts or as huge trees
or rushing waters.[22] The people of God and their leaders are
also depicted correspondingly as land or lion or vine.[23] The
beginnings of this codified language may already be found in
the Old Testament prophets. Isaiah describes Israel as a
vineyard, for example (ch.5); Jeremiah announces the coming
of wild beasts from the north to tear Israel to pieces (5.6). But
what is plain in the prophets - a transparently simple image - is
heightened into the grotesque by the apocalyptic writers and is
now incomprehensible without interpretation. The account of
Alexander's empire and the rule of his successors, 'Diadochi',
given in Dan. 7. 7f. belongs to the symbolic discourses which
can be relatively easily understood:

> After this I saw in the night visions, and behold, a fourth
> beast, terrible and dreadful and exceedingly strong; and it
> had great iron teeth; it devoured and broke in pieces, and
> stamped the residue with its feet. It was different from all
> the beasts that were before it; and it had ten horns. I

considered the horns, and behold, there came up among them another horn, a little one, before which three of the first horns were plucked up by the roots; and behold, in this horn were eyes like the eyes of a man, and a mouth speaking great things.

The apocalyptic descriptions suggest to many exegetes the suspicion that their authors were remythologizing the long-since demythologized religion - particularly since it is hard to discover how far such images are meant literally and how far they are intended to be pure metaphors.

The Semitic languages of the ancient world are invariably richer in symbols and more mythically charged than our rationalized modern European languages. To talk about an angel in heaven and the dead who sleep in the underworld, or about the devil who prowls around like a roaring lion, is nothing out of the way for a New Testament contemporary. There is not a single book in the Bible where mythical overtones are not to be heard or in which symbolic images are not used. None the less, the picture language of the apocalypses is so noticeable and so curious that it stands out clearly from the normal framework of the literature of the time and suggests a particular linguistic training, perhaps even a particular mentality.

(vi) All the apocalypses obviously have a long literary development behind them. The *composite character* is unmistakable - clearer than in other comparable literary works of the time (except, possibly, the late Mishnah). Breaks in the train of thought and contradictions in detail crop up everywhere. The book of Daniel even uses two languages, Hebrew in the opening chapter and chs. 8-12, Aramaic in chs. 2-7, thereby betraying its composite character in a particular way.

These outward characteristics would seem to be enough to allow us to view the apocalypse as a literary form current round about the turn of the era in the Hebrew-Aramaic linguistic area. If this is disputed it is because the linguistic structure is being ignored, i.e., it is a matter of different presuppositions, not of form-critical observations and methods based on linguistic history.

Yet from the outset apocalyptic presents a complex literary type which has absorbed into itself several component genres. Without a distinction between complex and component types[24] there can be no form-critical approach to these writings.

3. A preliminary demonstration of apocalyptic as a historical movement

A literary type is not only a matter of formal characteristics; typical moods and ideas are equally important.[25] These are also amply present in the books in question - and so markedly that it would seem justifiable not only to talk about apocalypse as a form whose *Sitz im Leben* we do not yet know, but also to presuppose something like a movement of mind; and it is this which is indicated by the collective term apocalyptic. The pointers which can be cited for this are not so easy to pick out of the texts as the form-critical observations just mentioned; on the other hand these indications of an intellectual movement have played a part in secondary literature for a long time. I will try to confine myself to what is largely generally accepted opinion today.

(i) The writings are dominated by an *urgent expectation* of the impending overthrow of all earthly conditions *in the immediate future*. 'Surely I am coming soon, Amen', proclaims the heavenly Christ at the close of Revelation. The same mood is noticeable in the other apocalypses. The hope of the speedy end of the world remains nebulous only where early figures such as Enoch or Abraham are the authorities for the vision. In all other cases it comes unmistakably to the fore. Daniel already expects only three and a half 'times' till the end of the world - in another passage, more precisely, 1290 days or at most 1335 (12.11f.). This keen expectation is especially striking in II Bar. 85.10:

> The pitcher is near to the cistern,
> And the ship to the port,
> And the course of the journey to the city,
> And life to [its] consummation.

The same feeling is inherent in the image of the drops which continue to fall for a short time after rain, and the smoke which follows the fire (IV Ezra 4.50). Anyone who looks forward so longingly to the imminent end of the world makes a fantastic impression on the modern reader. This impression serves as justification for the commentators who treat the apocalyptic writers slightingly and do not give them credit for any logical train of thought.

(ii) The end appears as a vast *cosmic catastrophe.* There is no need to list expressly the horrors pictured in the book of Revelation. In Daniel the reigning world power which is repressing mankind is found again at the end in an all-consuming stream of fire (7.11). The later apocalypses paint the age which preceeds the world judgment as a time of increasing horror.

> And it shall come to pass that whosoever gets safe out of the war shall die in the earthquake,
> And whosoever gets safe out of the earthquake shall be burned by the fire,
> And whosoever gets safe out of the fire shall be destroyed by famine (II Bar. 70.8).

> Then shall the sun suddenly shine forth by night and the moon by day:
> And blood shall trickle forth from wood, and the stone utter its voice (IV Ezra 5.4f.; cf. Apoc. Abr. 30).

The series could be continued indefinitely. Descriptions of this kind have been a determining factor in forming the common notion of apocalyptic and cause it to be represented as *pessimism.*

(iii) The end-time is closely connected with the previous history of mankind and of the cosmos. The *time of this world* is divided into fixed segments; the content of these segments has been predetermined from the days of creation and can be found alluded to in concealed form in certain sayings of the prophetic books.[26]

Numbers such as four, seven and twelve play a mysterious role. Talk about filled and bounded ages which tend towards salvation or disaster cause the apocalyptists to be reproached with *determinism*; but the behaviour of the individual is never accounted in these writings as being predestined towards good or evil - it is invariably only the behaviour of nations or epochs.

It remains a matter of dispute in this connection whether the apocalypses intend with their doctrine of time to depict world, or even cosmic, history as a meaningful process.

(iv) In order to explain the course of historical events and the happenings of the end-time, an army of *angels and demons* is mustered, divided into a hierarchy of orders; the leading powers even have their own names - Michael, Uriel or Belial, and Satan, for example. Earthly history, open to the sight of all men, is correlated to a supernatural and invisible history about which only chosen seers receive knowledge, through apocalyptic channels. Above all, the angels of the nations constantly intervene formatively in the events of the lower world[27] (whose decisive turning points cannot be explained by merely internal motivations), eager to promote the success of their own nations and to repulse the others.

In the future, with the beginning of the new epoch, the barriers between earthly and supernatural history will disappear and the faithful will join the good angels and shine like the stars in heaven.[28]

(v) Beyond the catastrophe a new *salvation* arises, paradisal in character. For this the remnant of the chosen people who have kept their faith in their God and remained true to their religion will be saved. Others will partake of it through resurrection.[29] The return of creation and the time of Moses or David (the heavenly Jerusalem) is comprehended in the scheme *primal period - end time;* i.e., the beginnings return in the Last Days.[30]

The members of the non-Israelite nations will also partake of the coming salvation. Every apocalypse expresses anxiety for the whole of mankind, although this is individually not easy to distinguish from the particular redemption of Israel, which still remains a special one. A tendency to *universalism* is, however, unmistakable when compared, for example, with the future hope of the pre-exilic prophets or the views of the later Talmudic writings.

On the other hand, within Israel itself a distinction is made; it is no longer the people as a whole who are the heirs of eschatological salvation. Rather, the righteous in Israel are divided from the ungodly. The idea of the remnant of the chosen people which alone will be saved (a notion in evidence from Isaiah onwards) plays a great part. This differentiation has led to the apocalyptists' being today occasionally reproached with *individualism*.

(vi) The transition from disaster to final redemption is expected to take place by means of an act issuing from *the throne of God*. For this purpose God will solemnly ascend his throne or even permit that throne to be ascended by the Son of man.[31] From thence the final event will be initiated. Through this event the division between heavenly and earthly history will be abolished, the divine glory will appear and everything which is hidden will be revealed. This final ascent of the throne is a relatively old idea, which can already be demonstrated at the pre-apocalyptic stage in Isaiah 24.23; it can be explained by the fact that the throne is viewed as the indispensable foundation of sovereignty.

The consequence of this ascent of the throne is that the *kingdom of God* becomes visible on earth (Dan. 7.14; Enoch 41; Rev. 11.15), replacing all earthly empires for ever. In later apocalyptic the newly beginning age of the world, the age directly ruled by God, is designated as the age, or aeon, which is to come (IV Ezra; II Baruch). Because of the 'aeon' idea, it is customary to ascribe *dualism* to the apocalyptic writers, i.e., the conviction of a complete discontinuity between this evil world and that other good one. People then go on to conclude that the apocalyptic writers are not interested in the present world, let alone past history, emphasizing them at most as a dark foil to the radiance of the future, which alone enthrals them. It is questionable, however, whether the 'aeon' concept really has the purpose of emphasizing the 'wholly other' character of the future age of the world. It is all too easily overlooked that the kingdom of God, or the future aeon, is undoubtedly thought of as being already present, though in concealed form (Dan. 3.33.; IV Ezra 26ff.; Rev. 1.9).[32] The kingdom's final realization and manifestation in the Last Days is, however, clearly distinguished from its present hidden power.

(vii) As has already been indicated in connection with the ascent of the throne in the end-time, *a mediator with royal functions* is frequently introduced to accomplish and guarantee final redemption. But at this point the apocalypses diverge

widely in detail. The mediator has various names - for example, the Messiah, the Son of man, the Chosen One; and his function often differs as much as his title. Nor is it clear in many passages whether the mediator started out as an earthly person or as an angelic figure (e.g., Dan. 7.13f.). He is angelic at least in the Assumption of Moses 10.2 and in Dan. 12.1; and he is clearly human wherever he is called the Messiah. But in none of the apocalypses is God quite alone in what he does; it is never without some mediator or other that he brings about and eternally sustains eschatological redemption. The role of the eschatological mediator is particularly stressed by Christian theologians because of its christological interest.[33] For the apocalyptic writers themselves it is doubtless only a special example of the supreme role which supernatural beings as a whole play - not only angels and the just who have been taken up into heaven, but also efficacious forces such as glory, righteousness and wrath. This feature is often explained by the fact that for the late period God moved away into *remote transcendence* and that man's personal relationship to him thereby became so tenuous that religious feeling demanded intermediary courts of appeal. Where such an explanation is adopted it would seem only a short step to move apocalyptic into the vicinity of another spiritual movement, namely *Gnosticism.*[34]

(*viii*) The catchword *glory* is used wherever the final state of affairs is set apart from the present and whenever a final amalgamation of the earthly and heavenly spheres is prophesied. Glory is the portion of those who have been raised from the dead, who will thus become as the angels or the stars of heaven (Dan. 12.3; I Enoch 50.1; 51.4). Glory is then the mark not only of man, however, but also of conditions, the 'state' in which they live, the heavenly Jerusalem (Rev. 21.1ff.; II Bar. 32.4), or of the eschatological ruler (II Bar.30.1) who is above them. A bold man might conclude from this that the apocalyptic drama ends with a transformation of every social structure.[35] This is a remarkable difference from prophecy. Whereas the apocalyptic writers and pre-exilic prophets are at one in the conviction that the impending time of trial will bring with it the breakdown of all morals and order (e.g., Mark 13.12f.; II Bar.70; IV Ezra 6.21-24;13.31; compare Isa.

1.21-23; Jer. 5.1-3), opinions differ about final conditions. An Isaiah expects the restoration of a sound, feudally organized Israelite state and for Jerusalem 'judges as at the first, and your counsellors as at the beginning' (1.26). Jeremiah's eschatology is tantamount to the view 'that, in the land which at the moment is lying waste, conditions will return to normal and life will go on again.'[36] For the apocalyptic writers, on the other hand, the normal state ties and the judicature will come to an end; and work will become pleasure (II Bar. 73f).[37] With these expectations in mind, every commentator who is ill-disposed towards the apocalypses reproaches them with longing for a Utopia.

The eight groups of motifs which I have picked out can be shown to be distributed more or less equally throughout the various apocalypses. Nearly every one of them can also be found outside the late Israelite and early Christian apocalyptic. But the way in which they are arranged is characteristic of apocalyptic, and probably of apocalyptic alone. It presupposes that the authors understand the eschatological events *as a sequence* and want to show a continuous scarlet thread running through the whole. They are concerned with a divine manifestation to the community present at the beginning of the end-time. In this way apocalypse means not only the revealing of details (revelation as the communication of doctrine) but the disclosure of possible participation in the final and unique, all-encompassing coming of God among men. An apocalypse is therefore designed to be 'the revelation of the divine revelation'[38] as this takes place in the individual acts of a coherent historical pattern. But this never means a one-track systematic account, or a linear chronological one; rather, the *multiplicity of approaches*[39] always prevails as a matter of course in problems so important for the Semitic mind.

All this gives us the right to understand apocalyptic not only as a literary phenomenon but as the expression of a particular *attitude of mind*. The collective term apocalyptic, which came into use at the beginning of the nineteenth century,[40] can therefore still be retained today. We may define it with Ringgren as 'speculation which - often in allegorical form . . . - aims to interpret the course of history and to reveal the end of the world.'[41]

4. The position of apocalyptic in the literature
of late antiquity

Which of the late Israelite parties known to us from other documents belonged to the apocalyptic movement must remain an open question, in view of what we have already said about the problem of its *Sitz im Leben*. But it seems likely that these speculations were not enjoyed by the whole of Israel in this late period. There are numerous books of similar date which pursue quite different interests. It is at least difficult to discover any close relationship to apocalyptic either in I and II Maccabees or in III and IV Maccabees! And there are no apocalyptic traces at all in Philo's voluminous works.

In the case of many other writings the closeness to, or remoteness from, the apocalyptic movement is a matter of dispute. The Testaments of the Twelve Patriarchs and the Assumption of Moses can be assigned to the apocalyptic writings straight away, on the basis of the characteristics of apocalyptic eschatology already mentioned, even though only some of the characteristics of the type previously noted can be found there.[42] The matter becomes more difficult with the book of Jubilees.[43] A whole series of writings found in Qumran is clearly apocalyptic: for example the Book of Mysteries (QMyst), the description of the New Jerusalem (1.2.5. QJN), the Prayer of Nabonidus (4QPrNab), Pseudo-Daniel (4QPsDan)[44] and the Melchizedek scroll (IQ Melch)[45]. It is uncertain whether these writings derive from the sect itself or whether they were procured from outside. What has clearly been composed within the Qumran movement (e.g., the *Peser* on Old Testament texts or the War Scroll, IQM), makes the reader doubt whether he should plead for apocalyptic or not.[46] What is bound to rouse ever-fresh astonishment is the fact that it is impossible to point to any genuine apocalypse in the huge field of rabbinic writings, in spite of the eschatological themes which the rabbis also assiduously cultivated.[47] Not a single apocalyptic book known to us, with the exception of the Book of Daniel, is quoted by a rabbinic writer.[48]

If apocalyptic is thus one trend among others within Israel and its literature, there are, on the other hand, indications that similar ideas were cultivated outside Israel as well, leading to a literature similar to the apocalypses. A connection with Hellenistic *oracle literature* can be shown at many points. The relationship is obvious, for example if one examines the Hellenistic-Egyptian tradition about the eight-footed and double-headed prophetic Lamb, adorned with the royal tokens of the Uraeus snake and the ostrich feathers, which is said to have appeared in the days of King Bocchoris,[49] and which prophesied:

Nine hundred years completed - I will smite Egypt.[50]

Since Hellenistic oracle literature is largely based on eastern prototypes, the beginnings of late Israelite apocalyptic may perhaps also derive from Iran or from the Chaldaeans, who were active in Babylon and with whom the hero of the Book of Daniel is already brought into close contact. In view of the present state of research, however, it would be dangerous to draw fundamental conclusions from this relationship; for not only is the temporal and sociological emphasis of the Old Testament apocalypses still obscure - above all we are still awaiting an adequate study of the relevant Hellenistic literature, to say nothing of the Iranian.[51]

It has not been my intention to review apocalyptic literature in detail or to bring to light new scholarly results, although that is urgently needed. My aim has merely been to convey a rough impression of apocalyptic round about the turn of the era, before going on to a survey and criticism of the present discussion. In view of the throng of contradictory theories, it would seem advisable to narrow down the criterion of what is apocalyptic, rather than to extend it, and to insist on starting from a strictly form-critical basis.

Even with so cautious and restricted a view of what apocalyptic is, the themes we have indicated are still explosive ones, theologically speaking; for the effect of such an apocalyptic on the place of the New Testament in the history of ideas could have been considerable. Consequently Cullmann's recent suggestion[52] that the word apocalyptic should only be used 'in the neutral sense', as a mere term for literary types and themes, has little prospect of being generally adopted in the near future.

THE GULF BETWEEN PROPHECY AND APOCALYPTIC: GERMAN OLD TESTAMENT SCHOLARSHIP

1. Jesus as the continuation of prophecy

The heritage of nineteenth-century biblical scholarship has burdened us with a mortgage in the apocalyptic sphere; and it is only against this background that present-day attempts to determine the historical importance of apocalyptic can be understood. Without knowledge of the history of scholarship, no research can either be carried on or evaluated today in this difficult field. A brief review may therefore perhaps be advisable.

About the middle of the last century the Jena New Testament scholar Hilgenfeld declared for the first time that apocalyptic was the point of intersection between the two parts of the Bible. Only apocalyptic conveys 'the historical connection of Christianity with the prophetic predictions of the Old Testament.'[1] For a time Hilgenfeld's account was the subject of keen discussion among New Testament scholars, but it was unable to find a foothold in Old Testament scholarship, overshadowed as it was at that time by such mighty figures as Wellhausen and Duhm. The *literary-criticism school* to which they gave their stamp was based on the theory of a fundamental hiatus between Israel and Judaism - a hiatus marked by the Exile and the figure of Ezra. All post-exilic literature was assigned a lower status. Like many others, the apocalyptic writers are presented as imitators (*Epigonen* was the favourite term), who indeed developed the prophetic ideas but in a rather unfortunate direction.

The seed which prophecy sowed fell on no good ground.

It bore a double fruit, possessing something of the nature and spirit of prophecy, but owing still more to the ground itself: the *Law* and the *eschatological hope,* the law growing out of the demands made by the prophets, eschatology out of their threats and promises. With the assistance of external history, these two turned their people into the strangest people in the world.[2]

As regards the link between the Old and the New Testaments (a link by no means denied by the literary school), a view which may be called the theory of the *prophetic connection* was a matter of course. After a decline of five hundred years, Jesus of Nazareth - perhaps John the Baptist before him - picked up the thread of the great prophets, the series of which ended with Deutero-Isaiah. According to this theory,

> the God of the prophets at that point metamorphosed himself into a small-minded institution for salvation and correction, setting up a strict Jewish ritual law in place of a norm of righteousness valid for the whole world.[3]

This metamorphosis comes to an end with Jesus; the God of the prophets prevails once more, truer and more human than ever before.[4] Under Wellhausen's influence, the literary and religious developments which affected Israel's history in the New Testament period are described with acerbity by Schürer[5] in his three-volume account, a work which is still unexcelled today. It is significant for Schürer's assignment of apocalyptic to a lower order that in the first edition of 1873 he only devoted one separate paragraph to apocalyptic, and that this disappeared entirely in the second edition of 1886, being replaced by a general paragraph about the messianic hope.[6] What apocalyptic testifies to, according to Schürer, was the spiritual possession of the whole nation at that time and varied as much in content as the religious doctrines of the period in general.

The rise of the history of religions school and the development of form criticism round about the turn of the century did not make any lasting difference to the assessment of apocalyptic. It is true that Hermann Gunkel recognized quite early on that the theory of the prophetic connection does not do justice to the facts of transmission or the history of religion. He pointed to the significance of the pseudepigrapha and felt that the apocalyptic writings formed a complex of their own. Bousset and Volz tended in the same direction, the two contributing what are still basic surveys of apocalyptic along these lines.[7] Gunkel made a sharp attack on Wellhausen in connection with the status of apocalyptic.[8] But after 1900 the problems of the syncretism between early oriental ideas and Hellenism took on so overriding an interest for Gunkel and his friends that their concern with apocalyptic gradually died away; a form-critical treatment of the writings was never arrived at.[9] A sentence in a letter which Gunkel wrote to Gressmann on 21 June 1913 is significant:

> As a *student* I began an independent search for the explanation of the New Testament, convinced that it must be historically explained from some immediately previous phenomenon and not from the Old Testament. I studied the apocryphal books and in disappointment, the apocalypses, believing for a time that I had found in apocalyptic the preliminary stage which must be assumed . . .

Gunkel had therefore already left this stage behind in 1913.[10]

Then came the First World War and the renaissance of Protestant theology in the 1920s, which directed ideas into completely new channels. The exclusive interest in the Word and in the kerygma permitted the canon to take on a renewed importance and forced connections with the history of religions to retreat into the background as non-theological. In this way Wellhausen's theory of the prophetic connection became so much a matter of course that it is, for example, not even discussed but simply assumed without question in the relevant theologies of the Old Testament which appeared in the 1930s, written by W. Eichrodt[11] and L. Köhler.[12] Neither book has a chapter on apocalyptic at all. Research into apocalyptic in German-speaking countries stopped so completely that where treatment of the book of Daniel in Old Testament commentaries was unavoidable, or where the heading 'apocalyptic' had to be discussed in books of reference, foreign scholars had to come to the rescue.[13] The latest comprehensive account available in German is a translation of H.H. Rowley's book, *The Relevance of Apocalyptic.*[14]

2. The question of the apocalyptic interpretation of history

It was only after the Second World War that interest in apocalyptic began to show faint signs of reviving among German Old Testament scholars. One of the first to turn to the subject was Martin Noth, with his lecture of 1953 on 'The Understanding of History in Old Testament Apocalyptic', which has often been quoted since and may therefore deserve a mention here.[15] Noth pursues a particular question, namely the origin of the four-empire scheme which crops up in the book of Daniel. The title of his lecture suggests that he believes that the conclusion which he reaches is significant for the apocalyptic understanding of history in general: the four world empires are not mentioned and described because they follow one another in time; the round number four is intended to bring out 'that the coming of the Kingdom of God is always a matter for the whole of world history'.[16]

In the second part of the book of Daniel the attempt is made, however, 'to determine the actual detailed future course of history within contemporaneous limits'; but with this 'apocalyptic has deviated from its own starting-point and wandered off on a very dangerous false track';[17] Noth does not give any reason for his verdict. This essay is no doubt an 'occasional' lecture; it may be doubted whether a man like Noth would have been permanently content to reconstruct *the* apocalyptic interpretation of history in general from a mere two chapters of the book of Daniel - chapters, which, moreover, stand in contradiction to other parts of the book; quite apart from the fact that one may still have considerable exegetical doubts about Noth's thesis, even as regards these two chapters.[18]

The credit of having resumed research into apocalyptic in Germany once more is due to O. Plöger.[19] In contrast to the opinion current among German scholars in general, Plöger does not see the post-exilic period as being determined by one unified force, Judaism, whose members cherish one unified, vague eschatological hope. He rather distinguishes two broad trends, which are more or less opposed to one another. On the one hand stand the champions of *theocracy*. They see the goal towards which the divine path is directed as being fulfilled in the present religious, cultic and ethnological community of the day. The prophets have performed their task. This anti-eschatological attitude can already be seen in the Chronicler.[20] Sociologically the trend is supported by the priestly aristocracy. On the other hand there are circles which hold high the banner of prophecy, being at the same time open to Iranian influences. The supporters of this view were at that time in the minority; they formed conventicles and withdrew into an inward emigration,[21] seeking for the still unfulfilled 'goal of the way of God with man'[22]. Here apocalyptic developed along lines which can be traced in the written documents of Trito-Zechariah, via the Isaiah Apocalypse, down to Daniel. The theocratic community is not given absolute validity but is viewed as a 'link in the heavenly kingdom of Yahweh' which appears 'at the great eschatological turning point as an intrinsic part of the new aeon'.[23]

Shortly after the publication of Plöger's book, there appeared in the same series D. Rössler's *Gesetz und Geschichte* (Law and History).[24] Although this was really a New Testament thesis, its material derives mainly from the pre-Christian period; and for that reason we may consider it here. Rössler also aims to confute the theory of a unified (late) Judaism, his purpose being to make an adequate understanding of the New Testament possible. Whereas Plöger deals with the period between 400 and 200 BC, Rössler devotes himself to the period after 200 BC or, more precisely, to the period following the Maccabean rising. He too sees Judaism as being ruled by two conflicting tendencies, but he defines them, somewhat differently from Plöger, as apocalyptic and rabbinism. He does not illustrate the antithesis from the theme of eschatology or prophecy, but from the relationship to law and history. *Rabbinic* literature, with its beginnings in the work of the Chronicler and in I Maccabees, had no longer any living understanding of history, seeing it merely as a collection of examples of the true or false observance of the Torah, and the corresponding consequences. The law is given absolute validity and determines the conduct of life through its casuistry and innumerable individual tenets. *Apocalyptic* literature, on the other hand - particularly in visions - gives an impressive insight into the coherent progress of world history according to God's plan, from creation to the end of the world, a history which includes the whole of mankind. This survey of history becomes the basis for the understanding of man and the interpretation of sin and righteousness. Even the law, being the token of the chosen people, only has significance from the aspect of the divinely-willed history of Israel. For that reason it is not the individual commandment which is important but merely the law as a whole. Both Halachah and nomism in general are alien to the apocalyptists, unlike the Pharisees. Wherever the two trends converge (as they do in IV Ezra) a closer investigation shows 'the irreconcilability of Pharisaic and apocalyptic thinking'.[25]

Whereas Plöger's theses hardly came up against any exegetical criticism, but were also without influence, Rössler's investigation has often been attacked since on the grounds of its possible consequences for New Testament exegesis.[26] And the way in which the sources are selected to illustrate the two movements is, in fact, dubious. The apocalyptic texts treated by Rössler (I Enoch, IV Ezra and II Baruch) were written between 100 BC and AD 100, whereas the rabbinic texts on which he draws are several centuries later. It is rash to set the Chronicler or I Maccabees on the same level as these rabbis. Moreover, by about 1960 it was no longer admissible simply to bracket out the whole of the Qumran writings, which are also concerned in their own unique way with law and history. In addition we know a great number of other writings of the period which are neither apocalyptic, Qumranic nor, probably, Pharisaic and which none the less deal with law or history. Are these not to be taken into account? Moreover the interpretation of apocalyptic material is incomplete. There are undoubtedly paraenetic sections in the apocalypses where individual commandments are discussed, and considered as decisive for the evaluation of human behaviour - for example the worship of idols. Moreover the belittlement of the law in the interests of salvation history (in contrast to the absolute importance assigned to it by the Pharisees) is by no means clear in all the apocalypses. Yet none of Rössler's opponents has succeeded, as we shall see, in proving, as regards the basic themes of law and history, that there is a direct line from the apocalyptic writings to later, rabbinic-style Judaism. That in the apocalypse history has entered the picture for the first time 'as a unit and as a whole', with its 'basis in a predestined divine plan', through which every event acquires 'its non-interchangeable place in the sequence of time',[27] has often been contested since, but never confuted. Rössler is also right in maintaining that the omission of every reference to a Halachah and oral Torah in the apocalypses is curious, especially in passages where the material seems positively to demand such a mention (e.g. at the secret revelation to Moses on Sinai, II Bar. 4.6;59.4ff.). To this extent Rössler has succeeded in bringing out the independence of apocalyptic ideas on law and history, compared with what later counted as Jewish, even if the development of the distinction remains the task of future scholarship.

Soon afterwards (1960) the second volume of Gerhard von Rad's *Theologie des Alten Testaments* appeared, with a thorough-going consideration of the theme under the title 'Daniel and Apocalyptic'. Von Rad breaks with the practice of earlier Old Testament theologies of suppressing apocalyptic. The relevant chapter was even expanded in the 1965 revision of the second volume; with the exception of the beginning and end of the volume, it is the only chapter which was expanded to any extent, and it actually appeared separately as a supplement to the first edition. This shows the importance which the Heidelberg Old Testament scholar ascribes to the theme. Von Rad's interest is by no means guided by a special partisanship for this part of the Old Testament. It is, rather, probable that the discussion which has meanwhile arisen in New Testament and systematic theology has aroused von Rad's objections and has therefore moved him to a more detailed treatment. Surprisingly, von Rad coincides in his judgment of apocalyptic with his New Testament opposite number Conzelmann, with whom he otherwise carries on a violent feud.[28] In contrast, though he mentions Rössler and Plöger at the beginning of the chapter (n.1) under 'relevant literature', he does not refer to the content of their books in so much as a word, which one would suppose can only mean that he rejects their theses. Instead he bases his study on books written at the turn of the century and on their summary of the material, although he decisively diverges from them in their evaluation.

In the first edition, the *eschatology* of the apocalypses is treated first, summed up under the terms dualism, transcendentalism and esoteric,[29] which are not intended as terms of praise, theologically. In the fourth edition the section about the characteristics has been cut out; all that remains is a reference to a 'keen interest in the last things'.[30] Nothing is said about the positive contribution made by apocalyptic to the working out of a theological eschatology. The theme of the *resurrection* of the dead - so central in apocalyptic eschatology (and not only there) and so frequently treated - is completely passed over in the relevant chapter, von Rad merely mentioning in connection with Dan. 12 that it leads to 'an apotheosis of the Wisdom teachers'.[31] In the fourth edition the resurrection of the dead is mentioned once, in a list of features deriving from Iranian apocalyptic. Von Rad does not observe that it is a basic New Testament idea which is cropping up here.[32] The saying about the *Son of man* (which is also not unimportant for the New Testament) is certainly mentioned in connection with the book of Daniel,[33] but the question of origin and meaning remains undecided.

Von Rad takes the apocalyptists' interpretation of history more severely to task than their eschatology. They certainly concern themselves with historical material - with four world empires and indeed with world events in general, beginning with the days of creation. But Daniel already presents it 'from a spectator's point of view'.[34] The only appropriate term for this concept of history is 'determinism'.[35] In the first edition it is still admitted that the reduction of

> the endlessly varied shapes and forms of history to a number of relatively simple allegorical and symbolical representations . . . with some success . . . must be due to the ability of the writers of apocalyptic literature to reduce history to the primary forces at work within it.

The judgment of the fourth edition is quite different: now this incorporation leads to a 'positively hybrid-seeming universal Gnosis'.[36] Since the apocalyptists deliberately 'veiled their own standpoint in time',[37] it must be asked whether such a conception is not indicative of a great loss of historical sensitivity, whether history has not been excluded from the philosophy which lies behind this gnostic idea of calculable epochs; since here the experience of historical contingency hardly finds expression.[38]

In the first edition von Rad even talks about 'dispensing with the phenomenon of the contingent'. Not much is left, therefore, of an understanding of history.[39]

Von Rad is undoubtedly right in feeling the gulf between these writings and the history of the early Israelite period. For the apocalyptic writers never really did grasp the way to make contemporary history come alive. Even when they go into individual events, these are curiously schematically and bloodlessly linked together (e.g. Dan. 11). When they turn to early history, they exaggerate it recklessly, according to our way of thinking; we have only to think of the cosmological extension of the Flood and the covenant on Sinai.[40] The apocalyptic presentation of history with its total renunciation of imminent motivation, is far closer to the New Testament legends of Jesus than to the history of the books of Maccabees or Josephus, without ever achieving the fresh vividness of the synoptic narrative. Does this really suggest that the apocalyptists view history from an 'onlooker's' point of view? Such an explanation seems absurd in the face of the presentation of Antiochus IV Epiphanes in the book of Daniel or IV Ezra's struggle with the riddle of the destruction of Jerusalem.

Is it, perhaps, rather the case that the motivation of individual events has been forced into the background in a strained concern for the trend of history in general - that an eye for the foreground has been lost in concern for underlying relationships? In this case von Rad's second damning judgment about 'hybrid Gnosis' would of course seem all the more well-founded. But this judgment brushes aside the express eschatological reservation made by the apocalypses themselves (e.g. Dan. 12.9; IV Ezra 4.1-10).

A definition of the *spiritual origins* of the apocalyptists is associated with this evaluation. Von Rad is passionately opposed to seeing them as the successors of the prophets, widespread though this view is. For him it is 'completely out of the question'.[41] The only possible root is *Wisdom*, 'as regards material, the questions raised, and argumentation alike'.[42] The titles which the apocalyptists adopt, especially 'writer' (*sopher*), have now become for von Rad particularly important evidence.[43] The Wisdom character is also evident in the encyclopaedic strivings of the apocalyptic writings. There is no doubt that here von Rad is laying bare one of the important roots of apocalyptic - a root which did not appear at all in Plöger or Rössler. We also have reason to be grateful to him for expanding the list of Wisdom characteristics still more in the revised version of his book. But it had long been known that a considerable part of Wisdom tradition had penetrated apocalyptic.[44] What is new in von Rad is merely the exclusiveness of the linguistic derivation, the one-way street from Wisdom to apocalyptic and the denial of all inner contact with prophecy.

What is difficult about this is the apocalyptists' burning interest in eschatology. For, as is well known, the Wisdom writings of the Old Testament down to Ecclesiasticus have no eschatological reference whatsoever.[45] Von Rad escapes from this dilemma by a reflection which remains a question in the first edition:

> Can we not interpret this interest in time and in the secrets of the future shown by the apocalyptic writers in the light of Wisdom teaching that everything has its times, and that it is the part of Wisdom to know about these times?[46]

In the revision this becomes more definite:

> It involves no insurmountable difficulty, in our opinion, to assume that Wisdom (which was in any case tending towards the encyclopaedic) also, in a particular phase, probably a late one, developed a concern with the Last Things and that here also the absorption of foreign, and especially Iranian, material played a part.[47]

This information is of course both meagre and vague. We must agree with von Rad that the theological Wisdom of Jesus ben Sirach (Ecclesiasticus) in many respects resembles apocalyptic motifs to an astonishing degree; but then the radical difference

between this non-eschatological book and the book of Daniel -
written less than twenty years later - where eschatology is the
dominating focus, surely becomes the glaring problem. It is like
pushing a huge mountain aside with one's little finger. Anyone
who is not already convinced, for other reasons, that von Rad's
thesis is correct, will hardly be persuaded by his attempt at a
historical derivation. For eschatology is not simply added on,
as one additional theme among many others, which the
encyclopaedists can one day also come to include; it is the
absolutely dominating centre, round which all other material -
perhaps even 'encyclopaedic'[48] material - is grouped. How that
is supposed to be possible merely from the Old Testament
Wisdom known to us needs more cogent proof - especially after
Plöger's evidence of non-eschatological, but certainly not
non-Wisdom, movements. Moreover eschatology is not the only
stumbling-block in the way of a uni-linear Wisdom derivation;
we need only think of angelology and mythology in general.

Von Rad's account of apocalyptic cannot be detached from
the design of his *Theology* as a whole. Even this great work rests
on the theory of the prophetic connection, although this is
never stated. But there is a whole series of indications. In the
first volume the actual theology is preceded by a history of the
Yahweh religion. It finishes with Ezra. After that belief in
Yahweh has no further history: 'This Israel no longer had a
history, at least a history with Jahweh.'[49] The final section of
volume one makes post-exilic Wisdom merge into scepticism;
von Rad arrives at his conclusion by dealing with Ecclesiasticus
before Ecclesiastes, contrary to chronology. History is
similarly treated. Here the Chronicler's work comes in at the
end, in a mere seven pages. It shows, according to von Rad, 'a
dubious understanding of the law', quite apart from the serious
'denial of the realities of human life'.[50] Critical remarks of this
kind are not made about any of the pre-exilic and exilic
writings. Thus von Rad suggests to the reader that with the
Deuteronomic history and the prophets Israel's legitimate
tradition came to an end. It is only against this background that
the chapter on apocalyptic, and the passion with which von
Rad adopts his position, becomes understandable. Von Rad's
sweeping partiality is indicative of the whole predicament in
which German scholarship finds itself when facing the virgin

ground of the late Israelite period.[51]

Although von Rad's account raises serious doubts, even on a closer comparison with the apocalyptic texts, yet the book performed the valuable service of laying apocalyptic before a wider public as a historical and theological problem, and that in the most emphatic terms. Material which is otherwise only handled in narrow, specialist circles, is here at last brought to the attention of theologians in general as well as the wider group of all those interested in biblical material.

This achievement stands out all the more when one compares the other textbooks on the Old Testament. We have already mentioned the silence on this subject of the other theologies of the Old Testament. But even Eissfeldt's large-scale and reliable work, *The Old Testament: an Introduction,* while briefly introducing apocalyptic as the 'successor' of prophetic literature in the section on form criticism (though adding that the apocalyptists are 'no longer speakers, but simply authors'),[52] and while conscientiously listing the literary details even of the pseudepigraphic apocalypses, still does not know how to cope with their content.

> In view of the rich variety of these alien elements it is understandable enough that Judaism, when it had to fight for its very existence and was aware that its endurance would be possible only by the inspiration of its own powers, excluded the whole of the apocalyptic literature from its canon with the exception of the Book of Daniel, which had already been accepted.[53]

This basic view did not change at all between the first edition and the third.

Fohrer's recent revision of Sellin confines itself to the proto-canonical books and is therefore only forced to touch on our problem in connection with the book of Daniel. It is then explained to the reader that it is due to the 'sectarian character' of the book that it 'has been looked upon again and again by the apocalyptic and chiliastic sects as the focus of the Bible'. In the apodictic style which is peculiarly his own Fohrer then pronounces briefly: 'This view is due of course to inadequate study of this very Bible and is quite unjustifiable.'[54]

In his latest work on the Israelite religion Fohrer confines himself to two and a half pages on this theme; but they perhaps signal a certain change of front compared with the standpoint of the *Introduction*, the term 'sectarian' now being omitted and apocalyptic now being viewed as a further development of prophetic eschatology. Its intention is now summed up as follows:

> They (the apocalyptists) wanted to lift the veil from the mysteries of the End-time and offered disclosures of the waxing and waning of the ages of this world, so as to determine from that starting-point both the moment appointed for the end of history and the position of their own generation.[55]

APOCALYPTIC IN THE SHADOW OF PROPHECY: BRITISH AND AMERICAN EXEGESIS

1. Successors of the prophets, opponents of the Pharisees. The viewpoint of Old Testament scholars

It would seem advisable to devote a special section to apocalyptic research in English. As far as it is possible to command a general view of the situation from Germany, it would appear, astonishingly, that the exploration of apocalyptic was carried on under common presuppositions and prompted by the same questions in England and on the continent before the First World War; but that soon afterwards the ways of the Old Testament scholars parted and have not yet reconverged, even at the present day. Thus neither Plöger nor von Rad, for example, find it necessary to discuss contributions to the subject in English.[1] Conversely, in Russell's latest work, mentioned below, the monographs of Plöger and Rössler are not even mentioned in an otherwise extensive bibliography.

The investigation of apocalyptic in England is associated above all with the name of Robert Henry Charles, who devoted his labours to the subject to a greater extent than any other biblical scholar of the last hundred years. With remarkable creative energy, Charles produced solid textual foundations which are still unsurpassed today; for example Jubilees (1895), I Enoch (1906), the Assumption of Moses (1897), The Ascension of Isaiah (1900) and the Testament of the Twelve Patriarchs (1908). In addition he wrote solid commentaries, still in use today, on Revelation (1920) and Daniel (1929). Above all, he published a two-volume translation of the Apocrypha and Pseudepigrapha (1913), thereby producing a valuable (in places more valuable) counterpart to Kautzsch's German collection. In the introduction to this translation Charles sums up the result of his researches as follows: 'Before AD 70 Judaism was a Church with many parties: after AD 70 the legalistic party succeeded in suppressing its rivals, and so Judaism became in its essentials a Sect.'[2] Two trends come primarily to the fore in the pre-Christian period - an apocalyptic and a legalistic Pharisaism. Both appealed to the law, at least at the beginning. But the apocalyptic wing, which stressed the prophetic element, later passed over very largely into Christianity. It became increasingly anti-legalistic, even where it remained Jewish, as for example in IV Ezra. The two tendencies were moreover divided ethically by 'a great gulf'.[3]

It is hard for a German to judge how far Charles' views became general in England. An influential rival to him sprang up in the American George Foot Moore who in *Judaism* depicted for the late Israelite, Tannaitic period what he called 'normative' or 'authentic' Judaism. From this point of view there was no essential upheaval before or after AD 70. Teachers of the law followed the same channels of thought from Jesus, son of Sirach onwards: apocalyptic, like the other pseudepigrapha, only represents a deviation which lost itself in the sand. In the third volume Moore appends a controversy with Charles, whom he reproaches, in connection with apocalyptic, with confusing 'a literary form or a conventional fiction with a kind of religion'.[4] Since the English, unlike German theologians, do not like to carry antitheses to extremes, Charles had already preserved a connection between his two trends by setting them both down as Pharisaism. Even Moore makes no exclusive claims. He willingly concedes a certain latitude and variation of ideas before 70 and admits 'that there is a sense in which apocalyptic as the successor of prophecy had never been questioned'; only, apocalyptic must not be declared the sole or main heir of the great prophets.[5]

The Unitarian minister R. Travers Herford took up an unusual point of view in his book *The Pharisees*. He divides apocalyptic literature far more sharply from its Pharisaic counterpart than Charles. Although both are the children of prophecy, the one is a Jacob, the other (apocalyptic) an Esau.[6] The apocalyptic writings belong to the extreme Zealot wing -

people who through such literature were promptly impelled to their doom. 'Apocalyptic is full of promises, but it has never kept one of them.'[7] Even the late IV Ezra has nothing Pharisaic about it:

> The Pharisees had their faults, doubtless; but they stood for nobler ideas than these. Truly, their fate has been a hard one, at the hands of the world. Not alone have they been branded for nineteen centuries as hypocrites, but they have been made to bear the blame of all that is repulsive in Apocalyptic writings, whose whole spirit was repugnant to them.[8]

Charles' influence seems to have remained dominant in England. Research into apocalyptic remained a task for Old Testament scholars. British scholars especially have devoted themselves to an exhaustive philological investigation of the texts, but have also concerned themselves with the historical position of the underlying movement. It is impossible to list the numerous contributions made here.[9] H.H. Rowley tried to sum up the results in 1944 in his book *The Relevance of Apocalyptic,* which has already been mentioned. It is not by chance that he did this at the end of the Second World War. Rowley lays great stress on the unity of apocalyptic and prophecy. After a slow eclipse, the spirit of the prophets burned bright once more in the Hellenistic period, even going beyond prophecy at important points: 'The prophets foretold the future that should arise out of the present, while the apocalyptists foretold the future that should break into the present.'[10] A second important element besides the prophets is of course the foreign, and especially the Persian, influence. But apocalyptic 'owes more to the circumstances that gave it birth in the Maccabean age'.[11] Rowley describes each apocalypse individually, with a wealth of literary details, summing up the result in his final chapter, 'The Enduring Message of Apocalyptic'. A whole series of basic religious principles, valid for all time, found their expression in these writings for the first time. That is true, for one thing, of the idea of the *divine direction of the whole of history.* The pattern of divisions into four, seven or twelve ages of predestined time are for us a thing of the past. But one thing still remains: God is in control of history and at its decisive points history even proceeds from

God's initiative. Further: *there is a future for us and for our society,* which will leave behind it everything which has been in existence up to that point. But this future does not issue from human energy but from God's conferring grace. Longing for the Second Coming may no longer concern us, but the apocalyptic hope remains. 'I find nothing inherently unreasonable in this faith of the apocalyptists.'[12]The optimistic expectation of the future stands in contrast to a pessimistic evaluation of the present. 'The deepest *tragedy of evil* is that through the very ills it brings on men it breeds itself anew.'[13] That is why for the apocalyptists the time of this present world is ruled by devils and demons, who manifest themselves in great institutions and political units. Whoever is faithful to God therefore inevitably belongs to the oppressed, the scorned and the persecuted. Rowley finds the idea of a personal devil out of date, but not the idea of an impersonal force of evil in general. 'In all our sin we are not merely ourselves sinning. We are contributing something to the vitality of Beliar.'[14] The apocalyptists derive from this 'enduring ethical and spiritual principles of conduct', and awake in the individual the *expectation of eternal life.* Thus it is to them 'that we owe our hope of the Hereafter' - faith in the resurrection particularly - and, finally, the *Last Judgment,* with its important idea 'that life is charged with responsibility'.[15] Whatever one may think of the book's cautious attempt to distinguish between ephemeral and enduringly valid apocalyptic assertions - anyone who compares Rowley's book with von Rad's account of apocalyptic will have enviously to admit that in the attempt to penetrate theologically into apocalyptic, British Old Testament scholars are well in advance of German ones, just as they are in the philological field.

In England Rowley's position has up to now not been challenged in essentials - at least as regards the historical position of apocalyptic. The same basic ideas about the connection between prophecy and apocalyptic recur in S.B. Frost's *Old Testament Apocalyptic* and in D.S. Russell's *The Method and Message of Jewish Apocalyptic.*[16] But in recent years Frost has undergone a remarkable change of front. In 1952 he stressed that the apocalyptists saw their task in a *theodicy,* which they made good by means of a proof from the only medium of divine revelation which the Hebrews knew: history. 'If they did not always get their facts clear, they were at least the first men to essay a philosophy of history.'[17] Thirteen years later Frost supported the precisely opposite opinion. The apocalyptists have abandoned the historical thinking of ancient Israel and have invented eschatology by means of a new absorption of mythological schemes. 'The apocalyptists are in fact a school of biblical writers who recognized that the burden which Hebrew religion had laid upon history was greater than it could bear.'[18] Frost does not explain his change of attitude on the grounds of a deepened exegesis of the apocalyptic texts[19] but by means of a crude, black-and-white definition of what mythology is (aetiology, a supernatural world, absolute time) and through conventional ideas about the nature of apocalyptic (determinism, the dualism of the two ages, etc.).

Russell's book leans more heavily on Rowley but is also more thoroughly worked out. He brings out the point that it is useless to speak of a generally accepted orthodoxy before AD 70, or even of a dominant party whose beliefs represented the norm against which Judaism could be judged.[20] Like Plöger and Rössler in Germany but independently of them, Russell sees two streams as running through the late Israelite period - streams of equal influence, equal authority and equal claim to antiquity. The one, the apocalyptic, connects up with the prophetic; the other, the rabbinical, adheres to the law and the oral Torah, so that one can say with Sabatier: 'Apocalypse is to prophecy what the Mishnah is to the Torah.'[21] Whereas, however, the prophets expect the triumph of God to take place *within* the present world order, the apocalyptists emphasize judgment *beyond* time and history. At the same time the apocalyptic attempt strives 'to rationalize and to systematize the predictive side of prophecy as one side of the whole providential ordering of the Universe.'[22] Between the two characterizations of the apocalyptic viewpoint there is a still unclosed gap in Russell. For if the prophetic predictions belong *within* a world order, how then can the ultimate eschatological judgment - which is expected on the basis of prophetic passages - lie outside time and history?

Russell goes into the psychological background of

apocalyptic writing in detail, but that does not concern us here. What he has to say in the second part of his book about the apocalyptic message is a summing up of previous research. But the theological evaluation which clearly comes to the fore at the very beginning of his book is important. Russell maintains:

> Not only is [apocalyptic], in its teaching, a continuation of the Old Testament, it is also an anticipation of the New Testament. Christians believe that the New Testament is a continuation and fulfilment of the Old Testament, but the historical connection between the two, in respect of certain doctrines at any rate, is not always clear. The apocalyptic literature helps to bridge the gap and illustrates certain significant developments in religious belief, especially of an eschatological and messianic kind, which took place during the vital years between the two Testaments.[23]

2. Jesus ethical but not apocalyptic.
The position of New Testament scholars

British and American New Testament scholars seem to have undergone a remarkable change of heart with regard to the theme of apocalyptic and primitive Christianity. Whereas in the 1920s they took a strong apocalyptic infusion into account, in the middle of the 30s the mood changed. Typical for the earlier period would seem to be the following quotation from Burkitt:

> I venture to think we can go so far as to say that without some knowledge of Jewish Apocalypses, and a fairly clear realization of the state of mind in which they were composed, it is impossible to understand the earliest Christianity.[24]

William Manson's *Jesus the Messiah* may be taken as characteristic of the later stage:

> The Christian tradition of Jesus as Messiah and Son of Man has in fact nothing except the titles in common with the Jewish national and apocalyptic visions of the coming Deliverer.[25]

The title is only taken over in order to make clear the primarily 'ethical absolute' of the person of Jesus.

> It is of the essence of our moral experience that it, above all the determinations of our nature, demands an absolute for the full understanding of itself.[26]

But the primacy of ethic is non-apocalyptic. Jesus rather talks and acts in accordance with the awareness of God shown by the prophetic religion of the Old Testament. The English scholar therefore arrives at a theory of prophetic connection such as was long dominant in German research. It is not surprising that in this context Manson should refer to Eichrodt's 'fine analysis'.[27]

W.D. Davies' essay on 'Apocalyptic and Pharisaism' shows to what extent the changed attitude of British scholars has been brought about by German research and the usual continental stress on preaching and kerygma, as well as the rejection of doctrine and speculation. According to Davies there can be no question of Jesus' having belonged to the sectarian apocalyptic tradition, for three reasons: *(a)* Jesus' preaching primarily stresses ethics, whereas 'apocalyptic is not primarily concerned there-with;' *(b)* Jesus' eschatological ideas derive from the Old Testament, not from the apocalypses; and finally, *(c)* because Jesus was a rabbi, not an apocalyptic visionary.[28]

The origin of these arguments is plain. The emphasis on ethics is an English speciality; the theory of prophetic connection is imported from the continent (and seems to weaken the better British balance of trade of earlier decades!). Jesus as rabbi is an idea which is no doubt largely suggested by the gospel of Matthew.[29]

Since the 1930s English research has stressed the aspect of 'realized eschatology' in the preaching of Jesus. This is emphasized to such an extent that even so cautious and conservative a scholar as Oscar Cullmann can express his opinion thus:

> An exaggerated fear of attributing to Jesus statements dealing with final cosmic events can be found in the exegetical and theological writings of the English-speaking world in particular.[30]

There are still those in England who feel bound to Charles' heritage. Among these C.K. Barrett takes a pre-eminent place. In his collection of sources, *The New Testament Background: Selected Documents,* apocalyptic texts are extensively considered (ch.12) and assigned to a different section from the rabbinical ones (ch.8). Apocalyptic is seen as standing in the succession of prophecy and a 'widespread influence . . . in the period of primitive Christianity' is conceded to it.[31] Barrett's detailed views on this point can be seen from his short account *Jesus and the Gospel Tradition,* which also discusses German research in some detail. According to this Jesus thought of himself neither as Messiah nor as Son of God, but probably as a man associated with the 'story of an eschatological prophet who was exalted to heaven to be the Son of man' in the sense used in Daniel and Enoch.[32] The passion of Jesus only becomes comprehensible against the background of the apocalyptic view of the vicarious suffering of the Teacher *(maskilim),* who is already in Daniel closely associated with the Son of man.[33] 'If we cannot interpret the passion material in terms of "Son of man" . . . we cannot interpret the passion at all.'[34] As man in the pre-eminent sense he represents the suffering people. The resurrection and the coming again in glory are inevitably bound up with this view.

With this brief outline the thorny problem of the view of the suffering Son of man held in pre-Christian tradition is certainly not finally solved. German research is accustomed to react allergically to this theme; so it is not astonishing that a German reviewer reproaches Barrett with 'a historical combination which is hardly under methodological control'. But the insistence of German New Testament scholars on a 'precise analysis of form and tradition'[35] is a mere way of escape, so long as German research is not consistently at pains to extend such analyses to pre-New Testament literature as well, and in this case to apocalyptic. We shall see in the following chapter, unfortunately, that it is still far from doing so.

THE AGONISED ATTEMPTS TO SAVE JESUS
FROM APOCALYPTIC: CONTINENTAL NEW
TESTAMENT SCHOLARSHIP

From time to time, since the end of the last century, there have been influential representatives of New Testament scholarship who have considered that the New Testament, or parts of it, was influenced by late Israelite apocalyptic. A period generally follows in which apocalyptic's stock drops. The esteem which it has enjoyed within the New Testament exegesis of the last decades can therefore be presented as a series of waves.

1. The history of religions school

As we have already said, the first violent discussion about the meaning of apocalyptic was provoked by Hilgenfeld, round about 1850. But towards the end of the nineteenth century concern with the problem subsided again. Interest was re-kindled, particularly with regard to the New Testament, by the *history of religions school.* This school started from the presupposition that the Israelite - Christian religion, like all other religions, was a dynamic historical power, not a statically dogmatic one. The important thing therefore was to show in clear historical terms the road which leads from the late strata of the Old Testament to the early strata of the New. The theory of the prophetic connection was rejected as insufficient. In order to fill the gap between the Testaments, the apocalyptic writings, among other things, offered themselves. It was against this background that Johannes Weiss wrote his little book *Jesus' Proclamation of the Kingdom of God,* a book which attracted great attention. Weiss discovered that the concept of *basileia tou theou* (which was of absolutely decisive importance for the teaching of Jesus) is in content of apocalyptic origin,[1] and that Jesus took it over in the form into which it had already been moulded. This was a shock to many theologians at the time; for the term 'the kingdom of God', understood in a non-eschatological and spiritual sense, was greatly in vogue in Protestant theology and was held to be Jesus' uniquely original invention and a basic pillar of the Christian faith.

A few years later Albert Schweitzer gave Jesus a much more emphatically apocalyptic interpretation even than Weiss, describing the course of his life in dramatic terms in this light. In Jesus' utterances about the kingdom of God he sees 'the synthesis effected by a sovereign spirit between early prophetic ethics and the apocalyptic of the book of Daniel.'[2] Jesus' ethics, as these emerge from the Sermon on the Mount, appear from this point of view as an interim ethic - as stricter precepts designed for the short time of affliction before the imminent end of the world. *The Mysticism of Paul the Apostle* (the title of another important book of Schweitzer's)[3] can also only be understood on an apocalyptic basis. Here the Pauline doctrine of the necessity of dying and rising with Christ, as well as the Pauline ethic of redeemed existence, is based on the apocalyptic view of the kingdom of God. Schweitzer's theories, which attracted little attention at the time, were picked up by New Testament scholarship half a century later and after the Second World War turned the problem of the non-appearance of the *parousia* (the unfulfilled expectation of the end of the world) into *the* problem of primitive Christianity. Schweitzer was admittedly a lone wolf and had no direct connection with the history of religions school.

That school's representative in the New Testament field, apart from Johannes Weiss, was mainly Wilhelm Bousset, whose still indispensable book on *Die Religion des Judentums im neutestamentlichen Zeitalter* (1902) presents apocalyptic as one of the dominant tendencies of Judaism at that time, if not its dominating trend *par excellence*. Bousset was also an energetic supporter of the significance of apocalyptic for early Christianity. In his opinion, before Paul became a Christian he possessed 'an eschatological outlook such as we find, for example, in IV Ezra and the Apocalypse of Baruch'. Indeed, 'as is well known', the 'tense and acutely heightened expectation of the imminent End, which deeply determines the whole of the New Testament in its religion and ethics, derives from apocalyptic.'[4] Like other representatives of the history of religions school, however, Bousset shrinks back in the face of Schweitzer's radical theses and largely excludes the person of Jesus from this stream of tradition. Jesus' piety was only 'externally' at all related to apocalyptic and 'late Judaism'.[5] In the discussion which went on among New Testament scholars between 1900 and 1910, the themes crystallized out under which the relationship between apocalyptic and the New Testament is still considered in German research even today: Is there apocalyptic influence on: *(a)* the preaching of Jesus, *(b)* the outlook of the early Palestinian church, *(c)* the teaching of Paul and *(d)* even the theology of (the rest of) primitive Hellenistic Christianity?

Even at that time it became clear that there was a greater inclination to admit an apocalyptic stamp for Paul, and even more for the early Palestinian church, than for the figure of Jesus; although Jesus, both chronologically and in view of his *Sitz im Leben,* might in fact be expected to be nearer to apocalyptic than his later community, which cultivated a worship of its own. None the less, the *theory of a non-apocalyptic Jesus and his apocalyptic church* still enjoys great popularity today among such New Testament scholars as are prepared to allow the theme of apocalyptic a place in their exegesis.

2. The preponderance of rabbinic studies between 1920 and 1960

With the coming of the First World War apocalyptic ceased to be of topical interest. In the search for the background of the New Testament in the history of religion, the *rabbinic writings* pushed themselves more and more to the fore in the 1920s, as a fruitful source. The protean character of these writings suggests the notion that even the apocalypses are nothing more than one of many forms of rabbinic or Pharisaic theology.[6] Where the special character of apocalyptic was admitted at all, it was declared by scholars such as Jeremias, for example, to be the esoteric traditional property of the scribes, who were otherwise the public and energetic practisers of Halachah and casuistry.[7]

The conviction that Pharisaic and rabbinic piety was the dominant influence gained further ground through Strack-Billerbeck's immense collection of material;[8] here apocalyptic parallels were scattered among Talmudic passages and apparently fitted in without difficulty. Kittel provided theoretical support for this view with his book, *Die Probleme des palästinensischen Spätjudentums und das Urchristentum,* in which he expressly and decisively dissociates himself from Bousset's view. Kittel rightly criticizes the neglect of rabbinic literature in a work like Bousset-Gressmann, which purports to present the whole of late Jewish religion. But he now allows the pendulum to swing violently in the other direction. 'As the main line of post-exilic Judaism . . . only one comes into question: the "unshakable foundation" of the Law - and that for all periods.' Apocalyptic is merely a subsidiary type. Anyone who bases the history of the piety of the time on that is acting 'like a man who depicts the Christian life of the present day on the basis of the sects'.[9] For Jesus and primitive Christianity, therefore (since Jesus cannot for Kittel simply be classified as rabbinic), the result is a modified prophetic-connection theory, which is extended to the genuine, early Old Testament proper.

> Both Jesus and the scribes certainly have their roots in the Old Testament; but for Jesus this context was an entire one - the context of the whole of life . . . With Jesus it breaks through, not in the form of a few droplets, but as the full, living stream of the prophetic demand in its whole force.[10]

It is these convictions which lie behind the *Theologisches Wörterbuch zum Neuen Testament,* a work which like no other moulded the understanding of the New Testament for whole generations of theologians and in which apocalyptic is hardly given separate treatment at any point, even where from the angle of earlier research a more detailed consideration of the apocalyptic texts could have been expected. This pushing aside of apocalyptic is taken to considerable lengths: when the theme of 'the kingdom of God' is being treated in the article '*basileus, etc.*', *malkut samayim* in rabbinic literature is allotted four pages and it is noted that the expression is 'comparatively infrequent';[11] but not a single apocalyptic reference is cited, not even in a note! The same is true of *diatheke-b^{e}rit*, in spite of a section on the Old Testament apocrypha and pseudepigrapha.[12] For *dikaiosyne-s^{e}daqa* there is a section on 'Righteousness in the Synagogue', in which IV Ezra 8.36, at least, crops up in the middle of many rabbinic illustrations, with the observation that this idea 'stands on the margin of later Judaism'.[13] It is true that in the third volume apocalyptic is explained to the reader in one page, under the heading '*apokalyptō*, etc.'; but the opening sentence is significant: 'Judaism forged a certain substitute for living revelation in apocalyptic.'[14] There are certainly differences among the individual authors and there are articles in which apocalyptic takes its appropriate place. This is true above all of articles which appeared after 1960, such as U. Wilckens' *sophia*[15] and *huios tou anthropou*, contributed by C. Colpe.[16] But, as a whole, apocalyptic literature as a separate linguistic field is missing in this extensive dictionary.

Even where, in this period, salvation history was discovered to be the centre of the New Testament faith, and Jesus was stressed as the centre of the time between creation and the end of the world, as in Oscar Cullmann's *Christ and Time,* no one investigated a relationship to a possible understanding of history on the part of the preceeding apocalyptic. On the contrary: importance was attached to the fact that the New Testament view is 'radically different' from that of Judaism in its global aspect.[17]

In the New Testament field the declining preoccupation with apocalyptic was particularly marked in connection with Revelation. Ernst Lohmeyer's studies report for the years 1920-1934 is illuminating. At the very beginning he admits:

> There is indeed hardly a document in the face of whose stony reserve all methods of research - otherwise so frequently and so successfully put to the test - seem to strive in vain as, again, this last book of the Bible.[18]

The survey then begins, significantly, with research in English, above all with Charles' commentary.[19] The final section characterizes Lohmeyer's own point of view. He writes, among other things:

> One easily forgets one small thing: that the word 'history'

does not exist in the Old and New Testaments, but that its meaning is caught up in the mightier testimony of world and nations, world-time and the people of God; one also thereby forgets the greater fact that eschatology is not talking about far off 'goals', but about the Last Things, which are always the first things and the things of the present as well. In this abiding present-ness and actuality - God is *actus purus* - even a consideration of 'the whole of history' has doubtless its appropriate and restricted place.[20]

Was it this dogmatic position which forced Lohmeyer to talk about Revelation's 'stony reserve'? Still, he is so far influenced by the history of religions school, in his studies report, that he does not think that the origin of the book of Revelation can be found in rabbinic sources.[21] Accordingly, his commentary on Revelation, which appeared in HNT in 1926, draws so extensively on the late Israelite apocalyptic sources for explanation that H. Kraft, the editor of the second edition of 1953, notes apologetically in the preface that hand-written notes suggest that in later years Lohmeyer would have liked to make a more extensive use of rabbinic sources, and would therefore have granted another wing of Judaism its appropriate rights as well.

There were other New Testament scholars in Germany between the wars who continued to accept the validity of apocalyptic as an independent pre-Christian phenomenon, giving it an importance of its own for the New Testament, side by side with the rabbinic sources. Here Rudolf Bultmann must be mentioned first of all. He distinguished the nationalist hope of conventional Judaism from the cosmic eschatology of apocalyptic[22] and saw Jesus' picture of the future as closely connected with the apocalyptic expectation.[23] In statements such as these Bultmann's origins in the history of religions school peep through. Of course for Bultmann the preaching of Jesus belongs to Judaism, not to Christianity. As far as Paul and Hellenistic Judaism are concerned, these are dominated in Bultmann's view by a quite different influence, namely that of the Hellenized Gnosticism of the Near East, with its myth of the archetypal Man who is the Redeemer.[24]

In Germany the determining influence of apocalyptic on

Jesus and the whole of primitive Christianity has only been acknowledged by outsiders, and even by them only occasionally. For example, Rudolf Otto writes:

> Jesus' preaching of the kingdom is manifestly connected with (and yet . . . in definite contrast to) an earlier historical phenomenon, i.e. the later Jewish eschatology and apocalyptic. These constitute an extraordinary feature in the history of religion, and Jesus' preaching both reflects and transforms them. From the standpoint of the historical criticism of religion, his message must be described as one of their important forms.[25]

The early views of Ethelbert Stauffer were similar:

> The world of apocalyptic ideas is the one in which the NT writers were really at home. This proposition provides the required indication of the place of Christianity in the history of religion.[26]

But voices like these are lost in the great chorus of New Testament scholars who view apocalyptic of every kind with mistrust and discomfort, even when it appears in Christian guise, within the canon, in the book of Revelation. Even so cautious a commentator as W.G. Kümmel gives it as his opinion that 'there still remains no doubt that the Apocalyptist is in danger of falsifying the message of God's objective in world history.'[27]

This mood among New Testament scholars between 1920 and 1960 cannot be explained as being due to particular research results. For there was little, all too little, research into the history of New Testament times in those years, let alone into the apocalyptic texts. The onlooker cannot avoid associating the widespread aloofness from apocalyptic literature with the theology of the Word which was in vogue in those decades. Whatever the emphasis, whether on dialectical theology, the Lutheran confessional position or existential theology, all were at one in their ultimate conclusion: that the Christian kerygma has nothing in common with history and that church and world, faith and knowledge, lie on two completely different planes. This meant that every possibility of trying for a thorough understanding of the apocalyptic statements was excluded from the very outset.

It may be pointed out, as a postscript, that the Protestant attitude has by no means been outstripped through the postwar intensification of exegetical studies in our field in German Catholic theology. Even in 1966 it was still possible for so learned a commentator as Wolfgang Trilling to state: 'We may take it that modern research has positively established that the message of Jesus takes its bearings from prophetic eschatology and not from Jewish apocalyptic.'[28]

R. Schnackenburg argues more cautiously. He allots apocalyptic a separate paragraph in the framework of the pre-history of the New Testament and acknowledges its universal breadth, in contrast to rabbinic Judaism:

> The idea of the sovereignty of God and the joint rule of his faithful people is therefore retained, but is spiritualized and raised to the supernatural dimension.[29]

Over against these positive features, however, stand considerable failings:

> This dwelling on fantastic nightmares, this conscious excitement of anxiety and fear, this deliberate indulgence in an emotional expectation of the end of the world, coupled with the hammering on the theme of apocalyptic's secret knowledge . . . its concealment from the multitude and its delivery to the wise . . . the pride of the elect and the contempt for the *massa damnata* - indeed the positive thirst for revenge and pleasure in the destruction of the wicked: all these things are heavy shadows on the picture, otherwise so radiant, of universal perfection; and they are a blot on the apocalyptic writers who created them.[30]

Seen from this angle, apocalyptic is 'a flight into a world of visions and dreams, a flight, too, from a truly staunch faith, since what was demanded was tokens and calculations of the End'.[31] Jesus, then, stands in clear contrast to all this. He exalts the idea of the sovereign rule of God into the leading concept of salvation, understanding that sovereignty as 'a purely religious power',[32] to which everything political is alien. All his descriptions of the kingdom of God are, in contrast to apocalyptic, purely symbolical, 'which is the way in which a man must always apply them . . . to the things of eternity'.[33] It may be noted, incidentally, that Catholic Old Testament scholars do not search for their own view of apocalyptic either, but conform to the usual wholesale Protestant prejudices. Thus even a man like H. Gross, having stressed that the apocalyptists write out of an unshakable belief in God's truth, can write:

> It is hard to decide the extent to which they are using modes of expression borrowed from oriental religions; the ideas at least are almost entirely derived from the Old Testament. In contrast to the New Testament, however, this Old Testament material is degraded to the political and material level. Apocalyptic was therefore hardly a preparation for the Gospels; it led the people into national disaster.[34]

3. The effects of the demythologizing programme

If we are to understand the revival of the apocalyptic theme, we must be clear about the general situation of New Testament scholarship in Germany and Switzerland in and after the Second World War. The most important publication was unquestionably Bultmann's essay on 'The New Testament and Mythology', which appeared in 1941.[35] It was in this essay that he made the famous demand for a 'demythologizing of the New Testament proclamation'. The essay opens with the apodictic statement: 'The cosmology of the New Testament is essentially mythical in character.' It soon becomes clear that one of its roots is apocalyptic.

> The mythology of the New Testament is in essence that of Jewish apocalyptic and the Gnostic redemption myths. A common feature of them both is their basic dualism, according to which the present world and its human inhabitants are under the control of daemonic, satanic powers, and stand in need of redemption. Man cannot achieve this redemption by his own efforts; it must come as a gift through a divine intervention. Both types of mythology speak of such an intervention: Jewish apocalyptic of an imminent world crisis in which this present aeon will be brought to an end and the new aeon ushered in by the coming of the Messiah, and Gnosticism of a Son of God sent down from the realm of light, entering into this world in the

guise of a man.[36]

This mythology is outdated for every thinking person today, whether he is a believer or an unbeliever. It has become impossible for us to understand ourselves on the basis of a dualistic system of being. Consequently the apocalyptic complex of ideas is also inacceptable.

> '*The mythical eschatology* is untenable for the simple reason that the parousia of Christ never took place as the New Testament expected. History did not come to an end, and, as every schoolboy knows, it will continue to run its course.[37]

Apocalyptic therefore plays a central role for Bultmann, but in a completely negative respect.

Luckily, apocalyptic and Gnosticism do not sum up the whole of the New Testament. On the contrary, we can see

> a curious contradiction which runs right through the New Testament. Sometimes we are told that human life is determined by cosmic forces, at others we are challenged to a decision. Side by side with the Pauline indicative stands the Pauline imperative. In short, man is sometimes regarded as a cosmic being, sometimes as an independent 'I' for whom decision is a matter of life or death.[38]

It is the second group of concepts which still have a direct appeal to us today - man as an independent self, called to decision. It can be fitted without difficulty into the formal structures of the being of man, his authentic or inauthentic existence (as developed by the philosopher Heidegger). It will be the task of theology to interpret the first series of mythological New Testament statements in the light of the second, 'existentialist' series. This is what Bultmann calls demythologizing by means of existentialist interpretation. Wherever the New Testament talks in terms of a futurist eschatology (i.e., talks about an impending world catastrophe towards which history is tending), it is stamped by the mythological eschatology of Jewish apocalyptic. In Paul, however, this structure has already been heavily breached and in the Gospel of John it has decayed completely. Ultimately, what these mythical ideas mean to the New Testament writers is simply the existence of the individual believer in the state of 'detachment from the world'. Jesus makes this possible through the call of the kerygma. 'Everything in the world has become indifferent and unimportant [for the believer].'[39]

Bultmann's grandiose survey, with its incomparable tautness of reasoning, can now, a quarter of a century later, be explained in great part from the exegetical and philosophical situation of the time in which it was written. On the one hand, the eschatological ideas of the New Testament seemed to commentators trained by form criticism to an exact observation of the texts to be enjoying an ever greater esteem. Anyone who henceforth continued to see the New Testament as the basis of his faith and wanted to transfer its statements into the present in which he himself was living (and what New Testament scholar did not?) was bound to consider what the significance of eschatology was for that present.

It is not easy in the twentieth century to imagine an imminent end of the world at which angels fly down with trumpet blasts from heaven, while the sun is darkened and the stars cease to shine. Consequently many theologians felt it to be a liberation when Bultmann showed the presence of a quite different eschatology in the New Testament - an individual, wholly personal eschatology, bound up with the moment of truth - the eschatology of detachment from the world; and when Bultmann expounded this as being the real eschatology meant by Paul and John and the others. Perhaps one can also trace in Bultmann's scheme the ecclesiastically and politically desolate situation of the Nationalist Socialist period. There was nothing left for the members of the Confessing church (to which Bultmann belonged) and for many others who withstood the ideology of 'blood and soil' except a return to a personal devotionalism. This was certainly not a flight into 'inwardness'; the decision emphasized by Bultmann was authenticated by him and many like-minded people in numerous day to day cases. But it meant waiving the making effective of personal faith in public life - the requiring of reform or reformation through influence on institutions (which would also have been, in actual fact, impossible). In addition, nearly all discerning Christians had finally lost faith in a divinely willed progress in history after the outbreak of the Second

World War, particularly in view of the initial victories of the German army. This meant, however, that all apocalyptic longing for the speedy approach of the kingdom of God in time became suspect. (It is significant that in England at the same period Rowley produced a very different estimate of apocalyptic.)

The desolate years after the Second World War made Bultmann's theories seem even more convincing than before. Even when recovery set in, the mood continued to prevail for a long time; and individual devotion within the scheme of kerygma and decision was dominant even in quarters where Bultmann's demythologizing intentions were rejected with horror.

In the 1950s, under Bultmann's stimulus, there was a regular race among New Testament scholars with the aim of back-dating the scriptural evidence for demythologizing to the historical Jesus himself. Jesus was declared, with greater or less success, to have been a pure kerygmatic; he simply called men to decision. He was therefore, so to speak, the first theologian of the demythologizing movement and was as such the unique witness of faith. One may say that the renewed quest for the historical Jesus which set in about that time[40] largely derived its impetus from these ideas. It led to a general exclusion, from the very outset, of everything in the gospels which sounded apocalyptic as being alien to Jesus. This was possible by means of a method of reduction which was set up as a guiding line for synoptic research. According to this, the only sayings in the gospels which genuinely derive from Jesus are those which coincide neither with Jewish ideas, nor with the teaching of the primitive church. The only features which may be accepted as genuine are those which stand in visible contradiction to the directly preceding, or directly succeeding, periods. This method is consistently followed by Vielhauer, for example. Not only does he contest Jesus' use of every title (Messiah, Son of God, etc.) - that was already done by Bultmann; but he also denies Jesus' expectation of the coming of a Son of man, because that is too apocalyptic to be reconcilable with the sovereignty of God on the lips of Jesus.[41] Here the dogmatic conceptuality behind the demythologizing movement is acting as sponsor for the historical questions. For Vielhauer the idea of the Son of man contains 'objectivizing' (and therefore non-existentialist) aspects, in contrast to the *basileia tou theou,* which has as content 'strict orientation towards the kingship of God'; it was 'unburdened by apocalyptic and national expectations of the future' and is therefore the only concept which fits Jesus.

> In such eschatology the figures of the Son of man and the Messiah have as little place as have speculations about the time fixed for the End, or fantasies about the future world.[42]

This method of reduction suggests extreme historical conscientiousness. Is it not praiseworthy to work with a reliable minimum rather than with a multifarious maximum? The fascination of the principle for students and younger scholars is understandable. But the results are somewhat staggering. For what generally emerges is a picture in which Jesus is practically indistinguishable from a German kerygmatic theologian of the twentieth century. This suggests doubts as to whether it is really historical to lay down absolute discontinuity with past and future as the standard in tracing a historical personage and his influence.[43] It is not unimportant to point to this methodological question; for this is basically the way in which New Testament scholarship kept apocalyptic away from the person of Jesus for years, in order to link the demythologizing trend all the more closely with him.

4. The vexatious delay of the parousia

Since the beginning of our century it has become common practice in New Testament exegesis to sum up Jesus' eschatology, if not the whole eschatology of the New Testament, in the formula: 'now already - not yet'. This formula describes the specific and peculiar element of Christian faith, the point which distinguishes it from Israel and Judaism and thus also (and especially) from all pre-Christian apocalyptic. It makes it possible to comprehend Jesus largely from the aspect of the contrast with everything that went before. According to this view, the end of the world had, in the opinion of the New Testament writers, *already* come to pass through the coming of Jesus; at the same time, the daily

experience of every Christian tells him that it has *not yet*
happened; and it is therefore still expected as a future event.
The logical contradiction which is obvious in the formula
caused no difficulty in the decades in which a large proportion
of theologians strove to be 'dialectical'. Moreover, it must in
justice be said that the commentators were never content with
a mere formula but tried to explain it and at least to
authenticate it through passages in the texts. According to the
commentators, the parables of Jesus, for example, suggest that
the coming of the kingdom of God is still awaited. This
therefore shows a futurist eschatology. On the other hand,
however, Jesus says: 'If it is by the finger of God that I cast out
demons, then the kingdom of God has come upon you' (Luke
11.20). This is realized eschatology. If one wants to avoid the
idea of development - and that is what all the New Testament
commentators want to do - all that remains is the dialectical
information: 'All that does not mean that God's Reign is
already here; but it does mean that it is dawning.'[44] The usual
concept of the kingdom of God is given a new function in
combination with this kind of interpretation; the New
Testament *basileia,* it is maintained, must be understood
verbally and means the 'sovereignty' of God or even simply 'the
nearness of God', the 'being and work of God and . . . his
appeal to man and claim upon him.'[45] Spatial or even structural
features are therefore denied to the concept. It may perhaps be
a permissible question whether here the commentators'
disappointment with the 'German Reich' has not found an
appropriate expression and has led to the de-politicizing of the
basileia concept, so that its application to the inner life of the
individual becomes possible. The reinterpretation, which has
meanwhile become current coin, is not entirely reasonable, in
the light of the New Testament texts.

> It may fairly be asked what should the words of Jesus about
> a future 'entering into the Kingdom' and a future 'sitting at
> table in the Kingdom', etc., mean, if the Kingdom of God did
> not signify a world-order and a form of material existence,
> but only the 'sovereignty' of God, that is, 'God acting in a
> kingly way'.[46]

Where New Testament scholars expound the dialectical

formula *'now already - not yet'*, they do so in such varying ways, and the interpretations correspond so closely to the respective private theologies of the commentators themselves, that from this angle the formula itself becomes a dubious one.

> We must ask ourselves what effect Jesus must have had on his Jewish contemporaries, by whom he wished to be understood, if he had really intended and somehow expressed in his preaching the great variety of contradictions with which he is credited in the various modern interpretations of his eschatology.[47]

With these critical objections to the general way in which ideas are built up in New Testament studies, we come to the Swiss dogmatic historian Martin Werner who published the book just quoted in 1941 - i.e., the same year in which Bultmann printed his demythologizing programme. Linking up closely with the consistent eschatology developed by Schweitzer, this book carries the shibboleth of apocalyptic for the first time beyond the biblical field into the field of church history and the history of dogma. Up to that time the critical history of dogma had lain under the shadow of Harnack, who interpreted the process of the formation of dogma as the Hellenization of Christianity and as being far removed from the 'undogmatic' and universal gospel of Jesus, which preached the infinite value of the human soul. Harnack did indeed recognize an apocalyptic admixture in Jesus and the New Testament writers ('it was an evil inheritance which the Christians took over from the Jews'),[48] but he held it to be an ultimately unimportant husk which could easily be discarded. Werner denies that it is a husk which can be separated from the kernel of the kerygma.

> In the teaching of Jesus we find no trace of a new, universalist, undogmatic 'gospel' which might somehow have become linked to an inappropriate Jewish dogma about apocalyptic. Rather, in so far as this gospel is universalist, it is at the same time late Jewish in the sense of being apocalyptic eschatology, and in so far as it is in this sense late Jewish it is at the same time dogmatic teaching.[49]

What distinguishes Jesus from the apocalyptic before him is

really only the urgent expectation of the imminent end of the world. The kingdom of God, which Jesus always thinks of in terms of the future, will come very soon. The earliest primitive Christian community formed a group of its own in discipleship towards Jesus simply because of its expectation of this directly imminent end of the world, at which the returning Jesus was to act as decisive mediator. The events of Easter and Pentecost inflamed these apocalyptic expectations still more. This was the essential reason for the formation of a Christian church which separated itself from Judaism. But the parousia did not take place.

Consequently the Christian community had either to give up, or to take fresh bearings. It did the latter. The result was a step-by-step de-eschatologization through the development of Christian dogma. The Hellenization of Christianity, so much lamented by Harnack and others, was not the precondition of the growing alienation from (apocalyptic) eschatology; it was the result of that alienation.

This sketch not only traces back the rise of primitive Christianity to the highly charged apocalyptic elements in the message of Jesus (or to their refutation through the course of history); these elements are also made the determining incentive for the formation of dogma in general. Werner's outline did not make any essential impression on the histories of dogma. But it produced considerable disquiet among New Testament scholars. It is true that the consistent eschatology, and the interpretation of the kingdom of God hoped for by Jesus as being a purely future power, were unanimously rejected, and rightly so. For the New Testament statements are more complex than this; and no critical reader can be satisfied with an interpretation of the synoptic sayings which, like Werner's, ignores form-critical methods. Werner presupposes that there was a severe crisis in the first generation of the church - a crisis which must have brought the church to the edge of catastrophe; but for this there is no evidence in the texts. In spite of all this, the delay of the parousia became a subject which continued to fascinate New Testament scholars after the Second World War and, in close association with Bultmann's existentialist interpretation and his demythologizing programme, deeply influenced the spirit of research.[50]

But once the delay of the parousia comes under discussion, the apocalyptic background of the New Testament statements is bound sooner or later to become a matter of dispute once more.[51] And that, in fact, is what soon happened.

5. *The new advances of Wilckens and Käsemann*

Only a decade ago, the theme of 'apocalyptic and primitive Christianity' was vigorously taken up again in the positive sense by certain commentators who, though moulded by Bultmann's influence, had moved somewhat away from his Gnosis theory and had dissociated themselves from his existentialist interpretation entirely. The first contribution from this quarter was from Ulrich Wilckens. He starts from the statement: 'The riddle of Paul's conversion, therefore, is part of the far-reaching question of salvation history's turn from the law to Christ.'[52] How is such a reversal of direction historically conceivable in a man like Paul? It only becomes comprehensible if Paul was ruled, before his experience on the Damascus road, not by a rabbinical understanding of the law but by an apocalyptic one.

Wilckens bases what he says on Rössler,[53] according to whom the law in the apocalyptic interpretation had the salvation-historical function of preserving those who acknowledged it in the present aeon for the future kingdom of God. Where the law, in an apocalyptic scheme of history, possessed a mediating function of this kind, the encounter with the risen Christ was bound to lead to a revolutionary replacement of the law by the Kyrios - at least for so logical a thinker as Paul.

> Because the Christ event is completely and wholly *part of* the apocalyptic concept of the divine history of election, the primary consequence of the gospel of Christ is the radical *exclusion* of the law in its apocalyptic interpretation.[54]

In another essay published shortly afterwards, Wilckens extended to Jesus and the whole of primitive Christianity what he had here demonstrated for Paul. For Paul, according to Wilckens' view, the law was replaced in salvation history by Christ; he now traced this substitution back to the historical Jesus himself, as he is interpreted under apocalyptic premises.

The preaching of the coming *basileia tou theou* is simply the expression of the apocalyptic expectation of a final divine self-revelation. 'God . . . will demonstrate in his righteous judgment who he is, namely, the one who has elected his people', and who allows the righteous to enter into the glory with which he himself is surrounded.[55] Here Jesus assigns himself a decisive role, as witness the antitheses of the Sermon on the Mount, setting 'the authority of his own "I" against the authority of the Torah as it is understood in Rabbinic theology', which is only possible on the basis of an apocalyptic interpretation of the law.[56] This is certainly not a simple prolongation of ideas introduced by apocalyptic. 'A special, wholly contingent experience of Jesus must be presupposed for the establishment of a unique mandatory claim on the part of Jesus.'[57] But a certain continuity remains. At the same time there opens up 'a straight line from the claim of Jesus to the centre of the primitive Christian belief in the resurrected one', since the primitive church understood the resurrection as being simply, 'the divine verification of the claim that has been made in all of Jesus' behaviour'.[58]

In his fascinating exposition Wilckens is undoubtedly in danger of seeing the whole of Israel at the turn of the era as being apocalyptically determined. The Pharisaic and rabbinic movement, which was the great contrasting picture for his authority Rössler, recedes into the background; and in these initial observations he does not allow the Hellenistic diaspora any unique character. This is doubtless the only way in which we can understand how Wilckens can judge and interpret the whole of the New Testament writings in the light of apocalyptic. He criticizes the epistle to the Hebrews and the gospel of John because they depart from 'the apocalyptically stamped primitive Christian tradition' and detach the resurrection from its connection with the destiny of Jesus, so that, as an isolated 'exaltation', it threatens to turn into a myth.

> This could have resulted in the elimination of the entire Israelite, Jewish, primitive Christian understanding of revelation as the self-revelation of God in history.[59]

Wilckens' new definition of the history of the primitive Christian tradition from Jesus to Paul has been taken over by the systematic theologian Pannenberg.[60] It received little acclamation from New Testament commentators. The breach with seemingly established historical reconstructions was too radical; the new findings seemed too narrow and too simple; and Wilckens' fundamental theses about the apocalyptic view of the mediating role of the law in salvation history appeared to be insufficiently supported. Moreover the actual position of the Messiah and the Son of man in pre-Christian and early Christian apocalyptic remained open: it was still a question whether a line of descent could not be traced from here to the statements of Jesus and the primitive church. None the less, Wilckens performed the service of showing up the dilemma of current interpretations of the conversion of Paul or the origin of faith in the resurrection; and he also drew attention to points which are probably simply not to be clearly explained historically unless we take apocalyptic influence into account, however that influence be defined in detail.

A year after Wilckens, Ernst Käsemann published his essay, already quoted, on 'The Beginnings of Christian Theology'. As we have already said, the burden of his argument is that apocalyptic was 'the mother of all Christian theology'.[61] How does he arrive at this conclusion? Käsemann bases his argument essentially on the tenets of the sacred Law which he finds in the synoptic tradition and which go back to a pre-literary stage in the tradition. They postulate an eschatological *ius talionis*. Matt. 19.28f. is an example:

> In the new world, when the Son of man shall sit on his glorious throne, you who have followed me will also sit on twelve thrones, judging the twelve tribes of Israel. And every one who has left . . . brothers or sisters . . . for my name's sake [originally: for the sake of the kingdom of God], will receive a hundredfold [in this age] , and [in the coming age] inherit eternal life.

In sentences such as these a certain type of behaviour in this era is linked with a revolution of circumstances in the eschatological future. The present time is accounted wicked; the coming kingdom of God means liberation. The types of discourse in which expressions of this kind are to be found are eschatological promises, curses and macarisms - i.e., prophetic forms. Prophecy and apocalyptic, however, were closely associated at that time, according to Käsemann. Eyes are not only turned towards the future; on the contrary: the same level of tradition also strives to draw on the Old Testament history - that is to say, on the past - as a means whereby to illuminate the present, e.g., Matt. 24.37: 'As were the days of Noah, so will be the coming (parousia) of the Son of man.'

Here a peculiar *understanding of history* becomes evident. History proceeds unrepeatably in a particular direction, and is clearly divided into distinguishable epochs. The end-time and the primal period correspond typologically, the Old Testament being interpreted in an apocalyptic sense. The criterion and the goal is the parousia of the Son of man. This shows that 'it was apocalyptic which first made historical thinking possible within Christendom'.[62] It is not merely particular Synoptic sayings which can be explained from this viewpoint; the whole literary form of the Gospels has its origins in these premises, the story of Jesus' life being presented in the light of eschatology.

> Prophetic proof-texts and typology are the oldest testimonies to this narrative which is rooted in apocalyptic; as such, they determine on their side the proto-gospel of the Passion and, just as much, the genealogy and preface of Matthew, which, though late in their literary form, are nevertheless very early in the context of the tradition from which they came.[63]

Käsemann rectifies the current view, according to which the only concern of the apocalyptists was the final reward of the righteous and the punishment of the wicked.

> The heart of primitive Christian apocalyptic . . . is the accession to the throne of heaven by God and by his Christ as the eschatological Son of Man - an event which can also be characterized as proof of the righteousness of God.

That is why the Pauline doctrine of the righteousness of God and our own justification must also be derived from apocalyptic.[64] Käsemann traces apocalyptic ideas back to a post-Easter enthusiasm dominant in the primitive church, where the offices of the Spirit were decisive for the new Christian life, where the congregation was led by prophets (and hence charismatics) and where the priesthood of all believers was generally practised.[65] It is true that later theologians - Paul or Matthew, for example - had their hands full in fending off the dangers of an enthusiasm of this kind, but they remain anchored to the same apocalyptic foundation. Only Jesus himself can be set apart from this web of ideas.

> The situation was this: Jesus admittedly made the apocalyptically determined message of John his point of departure; his own preaching, however, did not bear a fundamentally apocalyptic stamp but proclaimed the immediacy of the God who was near at hand. I am convinced that no one who took this step can have been prepared to wait for the coming Son of Man, the restoration of the Twelve Tribes in the Messianic kingdom and the dawning of the Parousia (which was tied up with this) in order to experience the near presence of God.[66]

(Käsemann therefore makes the same reservation about numbering Jesus among the apocalyptists as Bousset and Gunkel did fifty years earlier.) None the less, Christian theology is permanently indebted to apocalyptic.

> This central motive was in fact the hope of the manifestation of the Son of Man on his way to his enthronement; and we have to ask ourselves whether Christian theology can ever survive in any legitimate form without this theme.[67]

For even Paul 'remained an apocalyptist even after he became a Christian.'

Käsemann has made a brilliant synthesis of his evidence and has sketched a thrilling picture of the vitality of the Christian spirit. Behind his exposition lies his own conviction, developed elsewhere, that the lordship of Christ is the central theme of the New Testament. What lies behind it in addition is the claim which he has been making for years against his preceptor Bultmann:

> I am not convinced that the ways of God are directed towards the justification of the individual alone. According to the New Testament, God's aim is not the salvation of the individual; it is the justification of the world.[68]

There is no doubt that it is true that the apocalyptic element in the synoptic tradition is much stronger than New Testament exegesis in general suggests. At the same time a doubt remains in the reader's mind whether the pre-literary apocalyptic stratum of tradition, extracted from Jesus on the one hand and from the gospels on the other, can simply be identified with the theology of the whole post-Easter primitive church. Nor does Käsemann explain how it was possible for apocalyptic thinking to stream into early Christianity on so broad a basis. Does he - like Wilckens - imagine the late Israelite period as being apocalyptically determined in general? Jesus' exceptional position as regards apocalyptic would then, historically speaking, be even more dubious than it is already. The theory of the non-apocalyptic Jesus and his apocalyptic church is taken to a new and almost unparallelled extreme. Käsemann postulates a double discontinuity - on the one hand to John the Baptist, and on the other to the early Jerusalem church; but it is difficult to imagine anything more improbable, especially since Jesus does not merely proclaim the coming of God (as did the earlier apocalypses of Daniel and Enoch from time to time) but invariably the coming of his kingdom. Moreover, Käsemann's concept of apocalyptic is not localized within the history of religion and rests much less clearly on the apocalyptic texts than is the case with Wilckens. There are unfortunately no signs of a community enthusiasm in the apocalypses themselves.

6. The reaction to Käsemann

Whereas Wilckens' theories found little agreement because they deviated too greatly from the well-trodden paths of research,[69] Käsemann's essay roused considerable unrest, especially among Bultmann's friends and supporters, among whom Käsemann may otherwise be numbered himself.

In the very next year the systematic theologian Gerhard Ebeling and the New Testament scholar Ernst Fuchs took up the cudgels against Käsemann.

The opposing position which Ebeling adopts is cautious but unequivocal in its trend. The title of his article is 'Der Grund christlicher Theologie' ('the basis of Christian theology'), indicating that the apocalyptic thesis touches the very foundations of theological studies in general. He writes on the very first page: 'According to the prevailing ecclesiastical and theological tradition (and especially that of the Reformation), apocalyptic is . . . at least a suspicious symptom, suggesting a heretical tendency.'[70] Käsemann is reprimanded for not making clear 'the way in which apocalyptic and enthusiasm (characterized, in the history of religion, as structural aspects of primitive Christian theology) are to be distinguished from, let us say, sixteenth-century forms, where the terms are applied in theological condemnation'. Above all, Ebeling regrets that Käsemann does not sufficiently take account of the change in apocalyptic ideas brought about by their association with faith in Jesus.[71] What is in the background is Ebeling's thesis of Jesus as a 'language-event', as the unique witness of faith. In this light the linguistic tradition which leads to Jesus is for Ebeling unimportant. He formulates the essential point as follows:

> For the basic framework surrounding the use of all christological titles and all kerygmatic interpretative schemata is this: that they only interpret correctly to the extent in which they themselves are capable of correct interpretation; and that means: to the extent in which the understanding which they bring with them can be corrected, or even breaks down entirely. What does the statement that Jesus is the Christ tell us if what Christ means is not disclosed in the light of Jesus?[72]

A sentence like this is astonishing on the lips of Ebeling. The notion that concept and interpretative schemata 'break down' when they are taken over into the Christian proclamation is otherwise a favourite argument in fundamentalist circles, from which Ebeling is conspicuously far removed. It is true that modern form criticism, with the light it throws on the history of tradition and *Sitz im Leben,* makes it possible to recognize how much the horizon of a stratum of tradition can be extended and altered through new historical upheavals; on the other hand, however, as soon as one considers form-critical methods more deeply, they make it inconceivable that a concept or the idea behind a verbal expression can 'break down', unless at the point where the basis of human communication is abandoned. Could anyone in the late

Israelite period really understand that Jesus was the Christ, if he did not already have a notion of what Christ was - a notion which could certainly be altered or, equally, confirmed through the encounter with the person of Jesus? The same question might be asked in connection with an eschatological expectation or an eschatological ethic.

But Ebeling does not only oppose Käsemann; he agrees with him in so far as he talks about the legacy which the initial, apocalyptically orientated christology left to all succeeding periods - namely 'in the name of Jesus to think of God and history together'.[73] Admittedly, Ebeling believes that to think critically of God and history together today necessarily leads to criticism of apocalyptic; otherwise the result is a 'Hegelian concept of revelation in universal history'. That this must be avoided seems to Ebeling to be a foregone conclusion. Instead, the result has to be 'that through the Word God shows his power over history by putting an end to history's power through liberation for his presence'.[74] Ebeling closes his essay with a four-page quotation from Kierkegaard, the quintessence of which is: 'Nevertheless the believer is nearest of all to the Eternal one, whereas an apocalyptist is furthest of all from him.'[75]

The New Testament scholar E. Fuchs expresses criticisms of Käsemann in his essay on the task of a Christian theology.[76] Rather like Ebeling, he sees as Käsemann's chief fault that Jesus as a person receives insufficient attention if either he or the creed of the primitive church is interpreted apocalyptically. Jesus does not belong within a continuous history at all; but in that Jesus 'through his example - giving Word *creates* history, namely that history which now takes place entirely between God and man', the world loses 'its power, which brings about the history of sin and death'.[77] Fuchs works with a concept of two times, maintaining that they are already present with Jesus himself and that they are not a 'concept' at all. The proclamation 'announces God's time to man and in so doing confers this time on man. Man now lives in two times, God's time and his own . . . And on the strength of this, theology *distinguishes* these two times and in this way holds our existence in them open.'[78] Where something of this kind takes place, theology (which is only then legitimate) ceases to be the promulgation of propositional truths and becomes a 'hermeneutical process which destroys the identification of revelation with propositional truths'.[79] Where on the other hand (as in Käsemann) revelation is turned into the conception of revelation, all that is left is law and judgment - 'the expectation of a fit of rage, so to speak, on the part of the universal Judge'.[80] The terminology of the New Testament may be apocalyptic but the thing itself is not. 'The apocalyptic terminology proves as much and as little in this matter as the miraculous material proves about the gospels' interpretation of miracles.'[81]

It will be no surprise to anyone that Ernst Käsemann did not take this attack lying down. His answer, 'On the Subject of Primitive Christian Apocalyptic', appeared in the following year.[82] In the very first note Käsemann points out that what he and Fuchs are disputing about is not some historical problem of interest to specialists; it is nothing less than 'the theological relevance of the historical'. The dispute gives Käsemann the chance for an impressive summing-up of his theories on the rise of primitive Christian theology. Jesus began with John the Baptist's burning apocalyptic expectation of the imminent End. He broke away from this, however. But his church returned, and had to return, to that expectation. 'We bar our own access to the primitive Easter kerygma if we ignore its apocalyptic content.'[83] The Hellenistic Christianity of the primitive period later transformed the apocalyptic heritage into a metaphysical dualism of the first and second Adam, the earthly and the heavenly seed, the 'sarcic' and the 'pneumatic'. But the fundamental idea remained apocalyptic: the pattern of the two ages. 'Paul's apostolic self-consciousness is only comprehensible on the basis of his apocalyptic.'[84] He uses apocalyptic traditions as an argument against the enthusiasm of his congregation:

> Man for Paul is never just on his own . . . His life is from the beginning a stake in the confrontation between God and the principalities of this world . . . As such, man's life can only be understood apocalyptically.[85]

It must be admitted that Käsemann's analysis of the development of primitive Christian theology is more concrete than Fuchs' as well as clearer historically. But the decisive point of difference - as Käsemann expressly notes - is not historical at all; it lies in the dogmatic premises. Whereas Fuchs thinks that not only proclamation but also theology must avoid devoting itself to propositional truths and ideas, and that therefore apocalyptic is barred on both counts, Käsemann is more than sceptical towards this position:

> It is true that in many places today theology is identical with hermeneutic. But preaching, confession and even hermeneutic without propositional truths, yes, even without 'ideas' - what would that be?[86]

Fuchs' objections to Käsemann's outline of the history of early Christian tradition and language were raised out of a linguistic-theological defence against all propositional truths. H. Conzelmann[87] on the other hand directs his attack from precisely the opposite direction, namely out of the conviction that theology has always to do with concrete, sober doctrine and that this was so even in the primitive church. Consequently he is bothered by the apocalyptic enthusiasm which Käsemann ascribes to the members of the primitive church. He finds a lack of exact evidence in the texts. What are to be found, however, are credal formulations like the ancient tradition in I Cor.15, which clearly pass on the faith in the form of doctrine: 'These, not apocalyptic fantasies or spiritual experiences, . . . are the well-spring of Christian theology.'[88] And (even more clearly directed against Käsemann):

> How precisely is theology supposed to have developed from apocalyptic, which was a bunch of objective ideas, and enthusiasm, which was a bunch of subjective experiences?[89]

Käsemann hit back in the same year. He censures Conzelmann's unhistorical approach but also his method of refutation by means of caricature:

> What seems to me dubious are attitudes which smack of the greengrocer's; the writer deals in bunches of objective ideas and subjective experiences as if he were selling radishes.[90]

Even Bultmann himself turned against his pupil.[91] He mounted no sharp attack, however, but secured his position carefully, admitting that there was considerable apocalyptic influence - influence which he himself thinks goes further in the case of Jesus than Käsemann allows. For Jesus, like the apocalyptists, reckons with the impending dawn of the *basileia*. In the case of Paul, however, Bultmann would plead for a greater detachment from apocalyptic. The eschatology of the present is more important for Paul than its futurist counterpart. Paul breaks through the two-aeon pattern by declaring the era of sin to be a preparation for the era of grace; this can only be understood in the light of his individual experience. Paul's theology and view of history derive not from apocalyptic 'but from anthropology'.[92] Contrary to Bultmann, it must of course be asked at this point whether a dualistic interpretation of the aeon idea is not here being presupposed as a matter of course, although it can by no means be definitely substantiated from the apocalyptic texts themselves.[93]

The hard and often seemingly uncompromising 'no' which Bultmann's pupils return to Käsemann's theses is surprising - partly because the inheritance of the history of religions school (which was friendly towards apocalyptic) was held high in the last decades by these very same New Testament scholars; partly because the wave of sympathy for Gnosticism (which perhaps meant that in some cases scholars lost their eye for apocalyptic, or at least could have done so) showed general signs of receding; and finally because Bultmann himself had always reckoned with a considerable apocalyptic infusion in the early Palestinian church. In his fundamental account of the subject he was still writing in 1964: 'The preaching of Jesus only differs from the apocalypses in so far as he does not give any picture of the future redemption to come, merely describing salvation symbolically as a great banquet.' The primitive church, Bultmann goes on, 'carried on the eschatological preaching of Jesus and enriched it by taking over some themes from the Jewish apocalyptic'.[94] It is entirely possible to develop Käsemann's theories from this starting point. But any such attempts meet with a storm of protest. The onlooker is bound to suppose that here it is the significance of the New Testament words for the present which are decisive, rather than historical observations. Anyone who finds a futurist eschatology impossible today does not want to find one in the New

Testament either, at least not exclusively. Anyone who is prevented by their historical sense from thinking in terms of salvation history finds it difficult to allow the New Testament writers to think in these terms either. For if, ultimately, something absolutely new is being expressed in Jesus and the church, Christian theology must appear as something new in the history of thought as well; its continuity to the previous epoch must then only be loose and intermittent. Perhaps this suspicion with regard to the anti-apocalyptists among German New Testament scholars teaching today is exaggerated and unjust; perhaps they are really motivated by historical objections to Käsemann's outline, which is at many points not substantiated. These reasons are most clearly evident in Vielhauer's survey of New Testament apocalyptic.[95] But if I am right, a far greater density of historical argument is needed, and less wholesale dogma.

But it is not only Bultmann circles which deny the theory linking the early church with apocalyptic. An equally determined defence against the ideas of Wilckens and Käsemann can be found in a man like L. Goppelt, though his defence is quite different in kind. As the title of his article[96] suggests, he views apocalyptic and typology as two mutually exclusive modes of mediation between the Testaments. (This is in contrast to Käsemann and many others who view typology as a method of interpretation which has had its strongest roots in the apocalyptic religious movement itself.)

> Apocalyptic interprets history as a sequence of events tending towards the End; typology sees it as a prefiguring of final events.[97]

What the New Testament writers, and above all Paul, aim to do is to see the Old Testament by means of typology as the mysterious precursor of the New. Here apocalyptic is merely the formal framework in which such statements are occasionally set.

> Unlike apocalyptic, Paul does not basically start from a picture of human history based on a theology of history; with the help of typology he rather outlines pictures of the history of election.[98]

Consequently, for our theological endeavours today, typology is the absolutely crucial category; apocalyptic on the other hand is more or less unimportant, if not positively dangerous.

7. Paul and Jesus against an apocalyptic background: Stuhlmacher and Strobel

In recent years a number of younger New Testament scholars, who are less weighed down by the exegetical and dogmatic problems of previous decades, have intervened in the debate. Their reactions to it diverge diametrically, however, so that an end to the schism between the supporters of apocalyptic and other New Testament scholars seems further away than ever. First of all two monographs must be mentioned which further develop the lines laid down by Wilckens and Käsemann.

What Käsemann had indicated about the apocalyptic background of the idea of the righteousness of God, was thoroughly explored by his pupil Peter Stuhlmacher. In a detailed exegetical investigation, Stuhlmacher rejects the widespread opinion that *dikaiosyne theou* was for Paul simply the pardon of the individual in the framework of a heavenly judgment. What he means is rather 'God's effective salvation-creating justice, which forms the world according to the divine standard' and which is realized through the action of the creative Word of God.[99] And the place from which Paul took the concept was apocalyptic. For in the apocalyptic writings (Stuhlmacher numbers the Qumran texts among them) the righteousness of God is 'the basic theological theme' in the sense of 'the enduring nature of God's justice, God's faithfulness and God's character as creator in a chaotic world'.[100] Like Rössler, Stuhlmacher stresses a fundamental contrast to the contemporary 'rabbinical and Pharisaic piety',[101] where God's character as judge is contrasted with his mercy and the highly charged implications of the salvation-creating divine justice are no longer recognizable.

In *Kerygma und Apokalyptik* August Strobel turns to the consciousness of Jesus, 'from the angle of apocalyptic interpretation'.[102] Jesus was an apocalyptist, for 'the direct immediacy of the expectation of God' is 'the real, fundamental content of the apocalyptic hope'.[103] According to Strobel, Jesus was conscious of himself as Son of man according to Enoch's pattern, and expected that he would presently be caught up into heaven and be exalted as judge of the world. It is part of this interpretation's premise that all Israelite eschatology was saturated at that time with apocalyptic; but that there were two trends - an active, Zealot trend and a pacifist, quietist one, both of which cut right across the nation and right through Pharisaic rabbinism.[104] Jesus, of course, belonged to the second.

The efforts of Stuhlmacher and Strobel show clearly yet again how shaky is the ground which is generally presented as 'late Judaism' - and how urgently work needs to be done on the pre-Christian and non-Christian material. The Qumran discoveries especially have revived the question of whether, and how far, 'Judaism' really existed before AD 70; and, if it did, whether that 'Judaism' was in any way a spiritual unity. How far can the positions held by religious historians, especially Bousset and Volz, still be adhered to? To what extent have the views of Moore or Strack-Billerbeck stood the test of time?

8. The return to earlier positions in protest against Rössler: Nissen, Betz, and Murdock

In a long overdue undertaking, A. Nissen, H.D. Betz and W. Murdock have again carried the angle of approach back from New Testament material to the pre-Christian apocalyptic itself.[105] They take Rössler's book (which we have mentioned above) as their target, seeing it - perhaps not entirely unjustly - as the cause of all the discord among German New Testament scholars on the subject of apocalyptic. By reassuming positions belonging to the pre-1959 period, these writers attempt to resist an exploitation of apocalyptic views in the interests of a modern theology of history - a movement which they believe was set on foot by Rössler's book. The three contributions differ among themselves, however, and their views are fathered by very different authorities. Whereas Nissen takes up Strack-Billerbeck's position, Betz and Murdock both revert in their different ways to the views of the 'history of religions' school.

There is no doubt that Andreas Nissen in his article in criticism of Rössler[106] displays an astonishing knowledge of the literature, although he is in danger of not being able to see the wood for the trees and only concerns himself in a cursory fashion with the textual meaning of the passages he uses. His controversial methods occasionally sink to rather a low level.[107] In contrast to Rössler's antithesis of an apocalyptic and a rabbinic view of eschatology and law, Nissen stresses the unity of rabbinic and apocalyptic ideas, though he admits that they are far from being homogeneous in themselves. There are already differences between the individual apocalypses, which are by no means less considerable than those between the apocalypses in general and the rabbis. 'Moreover the eschatological statements of the rabbis are just as confused as those of the apocalyptists.'[108]

There is no radical difference in the understanding of the Law either. The author of IV Ezra calls himself a rabbi and his book, like II Baruch, is saturated 'with rabbinic theology'.[109] Moreover Nissen apparently sees the Jewish understanding of the Law as being unaltered from that day to this. 'For the Jew it is not *what* it (the Torah) says and prescribes that is decisive, but who says it.'[110] Nissen is undoubtedly right in his assumption that even with the rabbis the point was not individual commandments but the will of God as a whole.[111] On the other hand, of course apocalyptic knew of indivdual commandments. Going far further than these considerations would allow, Nissen concludes from them:

> The presence or absence of Halachah in late Jewish literature is entirely dependent on genre and situation . . . Halachoth would be simply out of place in the apocalypses.[112]

Nissen further attempts to prove an explicit understanding of history among the rabbis by pointing to the salvation-history traditions which they used. Apparently Nissen counts every Haggadah narrative as a proof of an interpretation of history. He thus even arrives at the conclusion that the rabbis shared the Deuteronomic 'concept of history'![113] The same concept is to be found in the apocalypses wherever Israel is the centre of the whole historical happening, though this is simply irreconcilable with the scheme of the four world empires, found in other apocalyptic passages. This can be explained by the fact that, according to apocalyptic opinion, God has no longer ruled since the Exile; the forces of this world rule without him, and contrary to him. [114]

The very opposite can be deduced with as good - or better - reasons from the passages which Nissen cites as proof (I Enoch and Dan. 11.36); but the writer is little disturbed by small exegetical details of that kind. The scheme of the four world empires, taken over from outside, is characterized in addition by 'having absolutely nothing to say.' Here too Nissen can maintain his assertions so vocally because he does not reveal (let alone interpret) the text of the passages he is drawing on for evidence. Seen as a whole, Nissen is not concerned to expound a new view but to prove that earlier scholars (in this case the men of the 1920s) were right in their contention that a divorce between rabbinism and apocalyptic does not represent the facts of the case. Rössler's whole outline thus shows itself to be 'mistaken'. More exertion would be required, however, for others to be convinced by a 'proof' of this kind.

Hans Dieter Betz uses far fewer references to secondary literature in his article 'The Concept of Apocalyptic in the Theology of the Pannenberg Group'. [115] His attack on Rössler's position is not nearly so radical as Nissen's. He admits, for instance:

> I would say that the apocalyptists were the first theologians to discover that the relationship between world history and revelation has become a *problem*. Their dilemma has much in common with the contemporary problem as to whether there is any meaning in history. [116]

This does not prevent Betz in another passage (following von Rad) from asserting that the apocalyptists have 'dispensed with historical thinking'. [117] Above all Betz rejects any theological acceptance of these apocalyptic ideas. 'The apocalyptic solution of finding meaning for history in the order of the universe is unacceptable to us.' [118] But he agrees with Wilckens that Paul was strongly influenced by apocalyptic ideas. [119] Equally, 'it is one of the results of historical research that Jesus of Nazareth must be understood in the context of apocalyptic imminent eschatology',[120] although in both Jesus and Paul there are also features which have a different origin.

The objections to Rössler's *Gesetz und Geschichte* can basically be reduced to two. On the one hand Betz stresses that *world history* is not the central theme of apocalyptic thought.

> In his desire to gain knowledge the apocalyptist, apart from history, turns to the entire field of the ancient study of natural phenomena, especially to astronomy, astrology, demonology, psychology, botany, and pharmacy.[121]

Betz therefore regards it as certain that these spheres cannot be parts of salvation history. It seems to him a matter of course, needing no exegetical justification, that the word 'law' in the astronomical parts of Ethiopian Enoch is only used 'cosmologically', which is to say metaphysically and timelessly; Rössler deduces from this a false alternative.

> These passages, he suggests, do not speak of 'law' in terms of '*taxis* understood in the Greek sense' but in terms of 'a hierarchical system of angels', which safeguards the ordered course of the heavenly bodies.[122]

In the apocalypses the law of God is understood not only in the sense of salvation history but also cosmologically and timelessly.

On the other hand Betz stresses emphatically that apocalyptic is not to be understood as a development purely within Judaism, but must be investigated 'only within the larger context of the Hellenistic-oriental syncretism of the time'.[123] Rössler has to bear the reproach of a 'relapse into "Biblicism"'. Betz really does point to an important desideratum of research when he refers to the link with the literature of Israel's neighbours. But how the task of investigation is to be begun, methodologically speaking, remains unclear. The attempts made by Bousset, Cumont and Charles, which Betz praises, have as we know led to no uniform result, with respect to either the resurrection hope,[124] the expectation of the Son of man,[125] or the doctrine of the two ages or eras. An attempt to illustrate the intertwining of primitive Christian and Hellenistic ideas which Betz himself made earlier (on the basis of a single passage in the book of

Revelation, where an 'angel of water' praises God, 16.5ff.) did little to diminish the obscurity and failed to open up any basically new way of access to a theme which is central for apocalyptic.[126]

The American William R. Murdock chooses a different approach in 'History and Revelation in Jewish Apocalypticism ',[127] using numerous clear textual quotations, which one generally looks for in vain among German advocates of the same position. The dispute with Rössler and Wilckens, as well as with Pannenberg (their friend in the systematic field) is conducted from the angle of two apocalyptic themes, which make it impossible for history to take on a positive religious meaning in any way within these writings: one of these is the dualistic contrast of this world and the future eschaton; the other is the pre-eminent position of visions as a means of divine revelation. Rössler and Wilckens fail to recognize the generally 'dualistic understanding of history' because they also fail to recognize its religio-historical origin in Iranian-Babylonian astrological determinism, as this appears not only in the division into four, seven or twelve ages but 'with even greater perspicuity' in the doctrine of the two ways and the two spirits, which is expounded in the writings of the Qumran sect.[128] Murdock's train of thought presents a difficulty here; for the apocalyptic provenance of these writings is by no means so much a matter of course as Murdock suggests.

Reflections on the history of the tradition are missing in the essay. Thus Murdock mentions that the apocalyptic schemes of history do not cover the whole of world history, like the Iranian ones, but 'only the more recent course of history leading up to the eschaton'. He believes that the only possible conclusion from this is that the intention 'was not to promulgate a particular theology of history but to promote the certain imminent expectation of the eschaton'.[129] But is the opposite conclusion not equally possible? That the greater proximity to the course of events they knew which was characteristic of the Israelites inevitably made them assimilate the vast mythological schemes passed down to them more closely to historical reality? Especially when it is noted that the apocalypses do not simply start off somewhere in 'recent' history but, generally speaking, in the relatively remote history of the beginning of the Babylonian exile, choosing this point because the rule of the kingdoms of the world seen from this aspect meant the continuation of the royal rule of Israel.[130] In view of this modification, the thesis that, against the background of Iranian dualism, apocalyptic eschatology gazes, not towards the consummation of history but towards its complete antithesis, is anything but convincing.

The second part of the article is devoted to *processes of revelation,* according to the apocalyptic view. The apocalyptic writings view the present age as evil; although they recognize a divine manifestation in the midst of the present age, this is only directed towards a few select individuals, namely the men after whom the books of Enoch, Daniel, etc., are called. This could indicate a certain divine revelation *within* current history if the visions and auditions were true to experience. But they are not; this is shown in the first place by their pseudonymity, but also by the many ways whereby the divine manifestation is considered as being transmitted (heavenly books, dreams, a direct communication from God, etc.). This means, however, that these literary revelations of divine mysteries, being a highly provisional revelation in 'word and sign', stand in so complementary a relationship to the eschatological fulfilment in 'deeds and wonders' that all historical continuity between these literary mysteries and the future dawning of the end of the world becomes completely meaningless.[131] God therefore does not act in history. With regard to the frequently treated theme of pseudonymity,[132] Murdock accordingly assumes the commonplace modern view. Even if this were correct - and there is little to be said for it - it is still a question whether the apocalyptists do not also recognize, in addition to the visions which they themselves (allegedly) experience, an at least equally important divine activity in *external* history - as, for example, where they stress that in the course of the world God gives sovereignty at any given time to the person whom he chooses to have it (Dan. 4.22 and elsewhere).

The contributions of the last three years have brought no clarity but through their divergency have no doubt made the problem even more urgent than it was before 1965. If anyone asks why New Testament scholarship finds it so hard to arrive at firm conclusions in this field, we can only guess at the answer. It seems as if most New Testament commentators are tied to the Bible. Even if they firmly reject all biblicism in their private theology, they are still intensely concerned with the verses, and parts of verses, of the canonical New Testament, so that the outward glance is debarred to them. With untroubled consciences, scholars still draw on the apocalyptic texts, a sentence here and a verse there (as early Protestantism once did with its *dicta probantia*), even then only making use of handy translations. (It is worth noting that when Bultmann and his followers draw on gnostic texts, more account is generally taken of the context.)

Questions about the context, general trend, or the author's way of thinking are not raised. Commentaries do not exist; the need for them is not even felt. This is bound up with a second factor. The forms and language of the New Testament itself have been scrutinized times without number by its commentators. But even now the New Testament has hardly been brought into suggestive linguistic and literary juxtaposition with the late Israelite literature of the time, or with the contemporary Hellenistic writings of the East; for this literature is simply taken for granted, its investigation is not felt to be a pressing problem, and form criticism generally stops where the canon ends.

Of course commentators make numerous form-critical references to the Old Testament beginnings, comparing the sayings of the prophets and the wisdom of the book of Proverbs with the synoptic gospels, for example. But they behave as if the pre-exilic Old Testament literary types had maintained their position without dispute until the early Christian period - as if nothing had changed in their language, tradition and modes of thought in the intervening five hundred years. Even more does the *Sitz im Leben* remain obscure when neither language nor form is investigated. The neglect during the last decades of the history of the New Testament period (which frequently leads scholars to content themselves with an uncritical reference to Josephus as an authoritative historical source) then made its contribution towards turning the historical tangle of apocalyptic and primitive Christianity into an inextricable one.

The prevailing opinion among German New Testament

scholars is still that apocalyptic is a marginal phenomenon which undoubtedly played a certain role in some early Christian circles but which, seen as a whole, is unimportant. The textbooks which have appeared in recent years reflect this attitude in a significant way. Bo Reicke's study *The New Testament Era* contains no section on apocalyptic and only mentions it incidentally, in connection with the Essenes.[133] The fullest statement is: 'A venomous note was sounded against the Roman empire and the imperial house in Jewish apocalyptic of the Flavian period.'[134] In Kümmel's *Introduction to the New Testament*[135] the paragraph on 'Apocalypticism and Apocalypses' is inserted in the section devoted to the individual New Testament books, immediately before the book of Revelation. Willi Marxsen's *Introduction to the New Testament* is similar in this respect. In addition, when he is dealing with Paul, Marxsen resorts to the usual fashionable way of getting out of difficult situations by drawing on a modified form versus matter scheme.[136] According to this, 'Although we quite often find such apocalyptic material in Paul's letters, he himself was not an apocalyptist.'[137] Hans Conzelmann's *Outline of the Theology of the New Testament* contains no section on the apocalypses, not even on the book of Revelation. It is so insignificant that it does not even appear in the index of biblical references. The New Testament christological titles are treated without its being found necessary to refer to apocalyptic ideas. It is true that from time to time apocalyptic is mentioned, and Conzelmann presupposes that his readers know what is meant by it; but the tone is generally unfriendly,[138] and stress is laid on the difference between 'Jewish' and Christian apocalyptic.[139]

9. French reserve towards apocalyptic

As an appendix, the contribution of French scholarship to the problem of apocalyptic must be mentioned. This contribution is much slighter than that made by French scholars in other fields of biblical research. For this reason a hasty survey, making no claim to completeness, must suffice.

There are relatively few Protestant commentators writing in French and this makes it understandable that here the positions of German scholars have largely been taken over, although some of the more extreme features are thereby softened. We may take as a probably typical example the essay on 'Eschatologie et apocalyptique dans le christianisme primitif' by the well-known French New Testament scholar Maurice Goguel. No other scholar has since succeeded in developing the theory of the non-apocalyptic Jesus and his apocalyptic church in so moderate and well-considered a way as Goguel. According to this essay, Jesus derives from John the Baptist, John being an advocate of apocalyptic ideas but differing from customary apocalyptic in his preaching of conversion. Jesus later separated himself from John, and thus also from apocalyptic. 'Jesus' thought was eschatological, not apocalyptic.'[140] It is true that Jesus supported the idea of two succeeding aeons but that was a generally widespread idea at that time. He turned aside all the specifically apocalyptic ideas. The end of the world is never described; nor can it, according to Jesus, be calculated; rather, the Son of man will suddenly flash out like lightning from one end of the sky to the other (Luke 17.24). The 'central idea' of apocalyptic, however, the destruction of Satan in a final drama of grandiose sweep, has been superseded, for Jesus has seen how Satan has already fallen from heaven (Luke 10.18); his fall is therefore already a thing of the past.

The resurrection of Jesus impelled his supporters to return to apocalyptic and made them feel at home once more in apocalyptic ideas. But the apocalyptic element in Christianity is already reduced in Paul and in John the evangelist. In the later ancient church the idea of a world catastrophe apocalyptic in nature soon became religiously speaking defunct.[141]

Every page of Goguel's exposition is carefully thought out and builds up a homogeneous and certainly lucid picture of the past. If the solution is not convincing in spite of all this, that is due to the concept of apocalyptic which underlies the essay. Is the fall of Satan really the central idea of the apocalyptic writings? And was it not entirely in accordance with the understanding of the apocalyptic visions for Jesus to have perceived in such a vision the fall of Satan as having already taken place? The calculation of the end of the world plays a totally subordinate role even in some of the apocalypses, e.g. II

Baruch. There too, moreover, the Messiah, who rises in the Last Days, is described as a sudden flash of lightning, whose light fills the whole world (ch. 53).

French biblical scholarship is largely in the hands of Catholic scholars, who have been comparatively little concerned with the apocalyptic writings. It is significant that down to the present day there has been no French translation of the relevant texts equal in value in Kautzsch's German or Charles' English one. French scholars certainly devote attention to the world of the New Testament, but the lines followed are similar to those of the conservative German New Testament scholarship mentioned above.

The well-known book by the pioneer of biblical scholarship, the Dominican M.J. Lagrange, *Le Judaisme avant Jésus-Christ,* is, indeed, a detailed presentation of the relation between apocalyptic and prophecy supported by some valuable observations.[142] Lagrange sums up the spirit and teaching of apocalyptic,[143] also recognizing that the ideas of these writings about world history represent a preparation for the New Testament idea of the kingdom of God;[144] but he stresses at the very beginning that the attempted division of 'late Judaism' into different streams has brought research to a dead end and ought to be abandoned.[145] It is significant that it was Schürer's account which gave him the clue for his presentation of the history.[146] The Pharisees appear from the outset as the dominating trend of the time.[147]

Four years later the Jesuit J. Bonsirven published a further extensive work on the same subject. Unlike his predecessor, Bonsirven believes that there were many parties in pre-Christian Palestine - Pharisees, Sadducees, Essenes, popular movements and apocalyptists.[148] But this does not affect the plan of his book, especially since he discovers in works such as IV Ezra and II Baruch signs of a 'genuine Pharisaic spirit', and considers even the Assumption of Moses and the Testaments of the Twelve Patriarchs as Pharisaic, though 'somewhat pietistic in tone'.[149]

In the introduction to a French translation of the apocryphal books, Daniel-Rops describes apocalyptic as the successor of prophecy, but with an important reservation:

There was of course the essential difference that prophecy

rested firmly on reality and the present, since Israel's soul
could then view its hope as being capable of realization. The
apocalyptists, on the other hand, rejected reality, which had
become odious and unendurable, and consequently more or
less fell victims to the temptations of pure fantasy and to
morbid daydreams; unless indeed they clung to a hope which
was, in a curious way, an all too earthly one. . . . The Jewish
apocalyptists by no means prepared the way for Christ; on
the contrary, by extolling the idea of the glorious and
powerful Messiah (in the earthly sense), they played their
part in entangling Israel in the tragic error whose consequence was to be the crime of Golgotha. The heir of these
daydreams . . . is not Christ but Bar Kochba, the condottiere
of the final, senseless rising.[150]

In the past thirty years the value ascribed to apocalyptic has
apparently diminished even more rapidly in France than in
Germany. This, at least, is the conclusion suggested by a little
book by the Strasbourg New Testament scholar M. Simon.[151]
In 135 pages Simon not only deals with the Pharisees, the
Sadducees and the Qumran group, but also with Baptists and
Hemerobaptists. Apocalyptic, however, is not mentioned at
all! It is astonishing that French research, so zealous in other
respects, has passed so negligently over the theme with which
we are concerned. What is the reason? Perhaps Catholic dogma
plays a certain role, for these scholars. A French Catholic, it
would seem (at least before the end of the Second Vatican
Council), inevitably investigates Judaism under the heading of
legitimate tradition. He is looking for the 'tradition catholique
du judaisme', as Bonsirven once put it.[151] This produces an
attitude which is in principle similar to that of the old
heresy-hunter Hegesippus, who distinguished orthodox and
heretical movements in Judaism as well as in the church and
viewed the latter as illegitimate from the outset;[152] although
even in France people are no longer so naive as to attempt
simply to trace the Christian sects back to the Jewish
aberrations, as Hegesippus did. (Of course it is a question
whether many Protestant scholars are not similarly prejudiced,
whether they tend towards 'normative' Judaism, seeming
thereby to be all too predetermined by their own theology of

'pure doctrine').

But it must at the same time be stressed that it was a Catholic French scholar, Léon Gry, who devoted himself for over twenty-five years to the textual and exegetical problems of an apocalyptic book, thus contributing more to a genuine investigation of apocalyptic than anyone else in the period between the wars. He published the results of his work in two extensive volumes: *Les dires prophétiques d'Esdras.* The very title, with its adjective 'prophetic', shows Gry's angle of approach to this apocalypse. He rightly complains at the very beginning that the apocalyptic book is still a 'hidden treasure' and that people generally treat it only superficially.[153] His individual results, however, belong less to the sphere of theology and the history of ideas than to that of literary criticism.

SYSTEMATIC THEOLOGY TURNS TO ESCHATOLOGY

1. Non-apocalyptic eschatology between 1920 and 1960

After the First World War dogmatic theology underwent a revival in the German-speaking countries such as it had not enjoyed since the days of early nineteenth century Idealism. The centre of dogmatic consciousness was absorbed by the Word of God, interpreted by dialectical theology as kerygma and expounded in confessional Lutheran theology as law and gospel. The self-understanding of the biblical writings and their centre seemed to have been rediscovered at last, and the perils caused by such disintegrating phenomena as cultural Protestantism, liberalism, and the history of religions school seemed to have been overcome. For in both the Old and the New Testament was not the word of God the really essential thing - that Word which breaks in on men in exhortation and claim, law and gospel, demanding faith and decision? Was not the Word of God in the Bible the only mode of divine manifestation and therefore the sole revelation? Is any other principle of departure permissible for theology except the Word?

Our fathers in theology had such a powerful sense of the present power of the Word in its conferring of faith and its gift of the church that for them history completely evaporated, not only in their personal faith but also in the outcome of their theological reflections; past, as well as temporal future, disappeared from their gaze and became insubstantial. Anyone who at that time opened the Word of God experienced contemporaneity with the faith of the primitive church, with the biblical faith in God. The leap over Lessing's 'awful abyss' almost ceased to exist.

It was not that no one bothered at all about *the past*. Historicism continued its progress in the outworks of real theological studies and, in the form of historical-critical research, was theology's thorn in the flesh. But scholars imagined that it had been basically surmounted or that it would at least be permanently bearable in the future. In so far as theology concerned itself with history, it liked to interpret it as the work of a law, contrasted with the proclamation, as the work of the gospel.

The successors of Martin Kähler appealed to a 'supra-history', into which faith ascended. Others, influenced by existential philosophy, withdrew at the decisive moment into the 'historicality' of each individual existence and an act of free decision. By whatever means, the idea was that one could escape the tentacles of history by a virtuoso act of faith.

The concept of the *future* was not simply overlooked either. Since the beginning of our century and the discovery of eschatology's fundamental role in the New Testament, systematic theology had also been inescapably confronted with the problem. At first a purely defensive position prevailed: the whole of biblical eschatology was a contemporary husk which had to be stripped away from the true, timeless gospel. The experiences of the First World War, and the crises in society which followed, suddenly made the pendulum swing in the other direction. 'Eschatological' became a fashionable word in German. The swing has been traced in detail by Folke Holmström.

> World events have moved eschatological questions into the centre of theological thinking itself, whereas in the nineteenth century they were pushed to a remote position, way out on the periphery of the dogmatic field, methodologically forming a last asylum for a reproductive biblicism.[1]

'History becomes a cry for the eschatological gospel.'[2] Karl Barth, the great inaugurator of the new theological movement after the First World War, was already writing in *The Epistle to the Romans* in 1921: 'A Christianity which is not entirely and simply and wholly eschatological has entirely and simply and

wholly nothing to do with Christ.'[3] But it is always longing for
an eschatology which will free us from the history which is
experienced as a burden. Eschatology is understood against the
background of the 'endless qualitative difference between time
and eternity', and is assigned to eternity alone, being stripped
of all temporal character. The 'real content' of eschatology is
strictly differentiated from the 'varying content of the
apocalyptic ideas and speculative postulates'.[4]

The popular eschatological exuberance, which yet·wanted to
remain non-apocalyptic, was subjected to a critical
examination by the Swiss theologian F. Buri in a book whose
subject was 'the importance of eschatology for modern
Protestant theology'. All the modern talk about eschatology is
really nothing other than an attempt 'to eliminate the New
Testament's expectation of the imminent end of history'.[5]
Even at the present time a need for eschatology seems to exist,
but its true kernel is at all times nothing other than the will
towards life's consummation in the face of a contradictory
present. In the New Testament this always expresses itself in
terms of apocalyptic and the end-time.

> The apocalyptic doctrine of the aeons, with the universal
> and cosmic stamp which it bore, . . . seemed tailor-made to
> serve as means of expression for the ethical resolve of Jesus
> and his disciples for the consummation of life.[6]

For the history which followed, however, this complex of ideas
and concepts had tragic results, since the hope for the speedy
second coming of Jesus which it initiated proved an illusion.
Buri's opposition to the eschatology of dialectical theology,
which was then in vogue, is convincing and is in some respects
an anticipation of Bultmann's demythologizing programme,
although it lacks the latter's methodological stringency. Buri
thinks that he can distinguish between the form and the
content of eschatology in a very simple way,[7] so that
Schweitzer's 'reverence for life' remains as the ultimate
wisdom. His protest came at the wrong time and faded away
unheard.

Attempts at a completely non-apocalyptic eschatology
dominated systematic theology in Germany between the two
world wars. Consequently Bultmann's initiative in the

demythologizing programme mentioned above was no doubt the result of the historical situation in the theology of the German-speaking countries in general and not merely a personal inspiration: Bultmann finally completely condemned the futurist aspect of eschatology, declaring an eschatology of the present (i.e., detachment from the world on the part of the individual believing existence) to be the real kernel of New Testament message; and therefore, of course, the kernel of our present-day eschatology as well.

2. The revival of apocalyptic universal history: Pannenberg

But no one can scorn his past without paying for it. The historical-critical research which was pursued in Germany with such stupendous energy after 1945 necessarily kept the theme of history alive and prominent, and repeatedly raised the question of whether the postulated contemporaneity of the biblical kerygma was true. Of all the various, more or less historically motivated objections to the theology of the Word, Wolfhart Pannenberg's is the most important in our context, because it leads to an express acceptance, not only of apocalyptic ideas but of the total apocalyptic picture. With Pannenberg the renaissance of apocalyptic in post-war theology begins. It could not have come into being without Pannenberg's personal friendship with Rössler and Wilckens, with whom he worked for years in Heidelberg. Pannenberg sets out to overcome the discrepancy between historical - critical research and dogmatic theology by seeking to discover from the results of historical studies what the nature of history is and, once this has been discovered, by making that history the basic theme of systematic and dogmatic reflections. The price is inevitably that terms which had hitherto been prominent, such as 'the Word' or 'law and gospel', were relegated to a position of secondary importance.

The consideration of what history is, and how it can be recognized, leads to the conclusion that it only becomes comprehensible in the light of a final situation. The confusing multiplicity of chronological facts only forms itself into a consistent picture of the past from the angle of an ultimate

goal. But if the whole of history be under discussion - the path
of mankind as a whole (and only then does historical
scholarship acquire real meaning) - that goal cannot be looked
for in the present; it must be sought in a future which can be
described as the end and consummation of history. Each of us
experiences the present as a transitional stage; no one reckons
with the possiblity that the destiny of man has already reached
its final realization. But how is the future *goal of universal
history* to be so defined that from that point a reliable total
picture of history can be developed and that the description of
history is incorporated? Anything of this kind is only possible
on the foundation of Israelite-Christian tradition, which taught
our world to be conscious of history for the first time.
Christianity is therefore capable of drawing up a picture of the
future realization of human destiny, because the final
condition of man is *proleptically* anticipated in the destiny of
Jesus Christ, and in his resurrection in particular. In Jesus it
becomes understandable that eternal life is the horizon of all
human existence. Pannenberg's first essay, 'Redemptive Event
and History',[8] therefore begins with the programmatic
statement: 'History is the most comprehensive horizon of
Christian theology.' Being a Lutheran, Pannenberg, the
dogmatic theologian, sought for scriptural evidence for his
thesis. At that time most New Testament passages would not
do as proof, since the theology of the Word had taken
possession of interpretation of them to such an extent that it
seemed impossible to discover a historical conception in them.
Here the Old Testament offered itself as a foundation,
especially since the Heidelberg Old Testament scholar Gerhard
von Rad had, like no one before him, worked out the way in
which the Old Testament faith was tied to history. But in the
Old Testament writings, past or future history is always only a
part; it is never described as being the outline of God's whole
design or of his whole revelation or revelations. For Pannenberg
and his friends it was a surprising discovery that there were
books which confirmed their own programme in a remarkable
way in the little-investigated gap between the familiar Old and
New Testaments; i.e., in the apocalyptic books. That is why
Pannenberg remarks on one of the first pages of his essay that
'Jewish apocalypticism completed the extension of history so

that it covered the whole course of the world from Creation to the end'.[9] Pannenberg wanted to revive the universal apocalyptic interpretation of history and to bring it to bear on the self-understanding of historical scholarship.

By viewing apocalyptic as the legitimate heir of the Old Testament and the essential precursor of the New, and by holding this apocalyptic to be, moreover, dogmatically legitimate and even necessary, Pannenberg dared to take sides with a world of ideas which had been suspect ever since the rise of historical-critical research and for which no serious theologian had taken up cudgels in the history of modern theology. It was an act of extraordinary courage for a systematic theologian to make such a volte-face; and opposition inevitably soon became vocal.

The resumption of the apocalyptic programme is even clearer in an essay entitled 'Dogmatic Theses on the Doctrine of Revelation', in a collection edited by Pannenberg under the title *Revelation as History*. The very first of these theses discussed is imbued with the apocalyptic spirit.

> The self-revelation of God in the biblical witnesses is not of a direct type in the sense of a theophany, but is indirect and brought about by means of the historical acts of God.[10]

The second is no less so: 'Revelation is not comprehended completely in the beginning, but at the end of the revealing history', for the apocalyptic notion of the divine plan according to which the whole history of mankind runs its course was taken up affirmatively by early Christianity.[11] The picture does not militate against the position of Jesus according to Christian doctrine; on the contrary, the significance of Jesus can only be comprehended when he is understood as being that very end of history which apocalyptic promised. Jesus is the centre and hinge of world history, not merely for religious history and the history of ideas but also dogmatically; he is the fulfiller of all the promises of Israel and at the same time a unique new promise. For Jesus' resurrection clearly reveals the eternal life which will be the destiny of all men at the end of history.

At the same time, however, *the resurrection as an actual event* is the proof of the outrageous claim of Jesus, even before

Easter, to incorporate the only possible divine revelation. Even more than in the first essay, the resurrection appears as the decisive event, theologically, in the life of Jesus. The resurrection is so important for Pannenberg that he even demands proof of its factual nature from the historians. But resurrection is incomprehensible without its apocalyptic matrix.

> It is only within the tradition of prophetic and apocalyptic expectation that it is possible to understand the resurrection of Jesus and his pre-Easter life as a reflection of the eschatological self-vindication of Jahweh.[12]

The postscript to the second edition is even more unequivocal:

> The resurrection of Jesus supports our attempt at a new interpretation of the concept of revelation. It depends on the one hand on the fact that the raising up of Jesus implies a confirmation by God himself of his pre-Easter appearance and that the pre-Easter Jesus remained dependent on this confirmation, so that no position in regard to the pre-Easter Jesus and his message can be justified without regard to the cross and resurrection. On the other hand, the proper meaning of the resurrection depends from the beginning on its connection with apocalyptic expectation: for only in relation to this connection is the resurrection of Jesus already the inauguration of the expected end, which for the remainder of mankind is still to come.[13]

Occasionally Pannenberg allows the apocalyptic premise to become the main pillar of his whole dogmatics:

> This eschatological character of the resurrection of Jesus as anticipation in Jesus of the end-event, for our outline, is the foundation of its original meaning as revelation of God, since . . . in the apocalyptic understanding of history the revelation of God's glory (and therefore of God himself) was expected in connection with the end-event of the raising of the dead and the judgment.[14]

In the light of apocalyptic the resurrection was axiomatic, at least for the people of the time.

For Jesus' Jewish contemporaries, insofar as they shared the apocalyptic expectation, the occurrence of the resurrection did not first need to be interpreted, but for them it spoke meaningfully in itself.[15]

Pannenberg seeks to arrive at evidence for the resurrection and for Jesus' whole life as the divine revelation and the disclosure of human destiny *per se* (for our present day as well) by means of an anthropological proof. This proof takes as its starting-point the modern - and not at all apocalyptic - idea of man's openness to the world, and therefore sees eternal life as his ultimate destiny.[16]

This is not the place to evaluate Pannenberg's total conception.[17] His bold assertion that the resurrection of Jesus can be historically verified may also be left on one side. The question which must be asked, however, is whether the position of apocalyptic in Pannenberg's scheme is a tenable one - whether, that is to say, historical apocalyptic really developed a total conception of history viewed in the light of its end, a concept to which contemporary theology can appeal; and whether the resurrection of Jesus was axiomatic for those involved, in as far as they thought in apocalyptic terms.

As far as the first question is concerned, a genuine apocalyptic interest in history in general is widely denied.[18] But these denials are for their part so largely determined by dogmatic premises that Pannenberg's attitude (which more or less coincides with the views of Rössler and Rowley described above) may be accounted the historically probable one, pending proof of the contrary. Pannenberg has in fact renewed an apocalyptic concern, though stripping away all the mythical components and combining it with a historical scholarship unknown to the apocalyptists.

The theme of the resurrection is more complex. The resurrection of the dead is certainly an important stage in the eschatological drama, according to the apocalyptic view. In Israel the expectation of the resurrection was probably an apocalyptic invention. But the resurrection of a single individual, as this is reported of Jesus, is an exception which is bound to seem all the more singular when the preceding and succeeding accompanying eschatological phenomena are

missing (as Pannenberg himself observes). It is not surprising
that it is not clearly discernible from the New Testament
writings to what extent the resurrection of Jesus was
understood as being the divine endorsement of an
eschatological pre-Easter claim. Moreover, the link of the
resurrection of the individual - Jesus - with the resurrection of
all believers is seldom so explicit as in I Cor. 15.20, where Christ
is raised as the first fruits of those who believe (RSV: who have
fallen asleep). Pannenberg's conclusions are at this point bold,
to say the least.[19] To the onlooker it seems doubtful whether,
according to both apocalyptic and New Testament evidence,
the resurrection of Jesus can in fact sustain the weight which
Pannenberg's conception lays upon it.[20] Pannenberg is
probably right in his contention that the resurrection of Jesus
plays a far greater role in the New Testament than present-day
systematic theology would allow. It is also true that the New
Testament statements about the resurrection are incomprehensible without their apocalyptic pre-history. But in the
course of Pannenberg's assimilation of the apocalyptic theme
into dogmatic reflection, the resurrection becomes so much the
salient point and sole foundation of the Christian faith, and is
so much isolated from all historical before and after, that it can
hardly be supposed that apocalyptic support can be claimed.

Pannenberg's scheme is without question the only one at the
moment which makes it possible to assimilate theologically the
apocalyptic trends of the period between the Testaments, with
their view of history and their expectation of the end. It is only
from this point of view that we shall be able to allow
dispassionately for extensive influence of the language of
apocalyptic on Jesus and the primitive church; and that we can
do so without Christian theology's falling to pieces thereby.

3. Opposition to the world in the light of the apocalyptic future: Moltmann and Sauter

Whereas Pannenberg attempts to take the Christian past and
the historical character of the biblical teaching seriously,
theologically speaking, J. Moltmann undertook, in his
well-known book *Theology of Hope,*[21] to move the future
aspect of faith into the centre of systematic reflections once

more. Here too, just as where history is taken seriously as a systematic problem, the futurist angle makes criticism of dialectical theology necessary, although the result is not as radical as in the former case. Like Pannenberg, Moltmann discovers the burning actuality of apocalyptic.[22] He sets out to restore eschatology from its obscure peripheral position to its place in the centre of Christian dogmatics. 'To believe means to cross in hope and anticipation the bounds that have been penetrated by the raising of the crucified.'[23]

Moltmann does, however, remain faithful to the theology of the 1920s in so far as he sees hope in unbridgeable contrast to history in its usual sense. 'Hope's statements of promise, however, must stand in contradiction to the reality which can at present be experienced.'[24] It is for this very discontinuity that he appeals to apocalyptic. (He therefore relies on another wing of apocalyptic research from Pannenberg, since the latter leans towards those scholars who ascribe to apocalyptic an interest in continuous history.)

Though he is indebted to von Rad, Moltmann has considered the problems involved independently, as we learn from ch. II, § 7: 'The Historifying of the Cosmos in Apocalyptic Eschatology'. The merit of Old Testament apocalyptic is that 'the existing cosmic bounds of reality . . . are not regarded as fixed and predetermined things, but are themselves found to be in motion'. The apocalyptic writers penetrate considerably further than the prophets.

> If . . . in the message of the prophets the Israelite 'hope for history' was struggling with the experiences of world history, and if in this struggle world history was understood as a function of the eschatological future of Yahweh, so it is also in apocalyptic: historic eschatology is here struggling with cosmology and . . . makes the cosmos understandable as a historic process of aeons . . . Then it would not by any means be the case that in the apocalyptic outlook . . . history . . . is brought to a standstill, but on the contrary the now universal hope for history would here be setting the cosmos in motion. In a struggle of this kind eschatology naturally suffers serious losses. Yet we must not look only at these, but must also see what is gained in them. The

'universe' is no longer, as in pagan cosmology, a thing to be interpreted in astro-mythical or pantheistic or mechanistic terms as the sum total of the world and of our satisfaction with it. Instead, it splits into aeons in the apocalyptic process - into a world that is coming and one that is passing away . . . The whole world is now involved in God's eschatological process of history, not only the world of men and nations.[25]

There is no doubt that here Moltmann displays an insight into apocalyptic which is all too often lacking among the specialist scholars. It is understandable that for Moltmann apocalyptic is as indispensable a part of dogmatics as it is - from another angle - for Pannenberg. 'Without apocalyptic a theological eschatology remains bogged down in the ethnic history of men or the existential history of the individual.'[26] In sentences such as these Moltmann rightly suggests that apocalyptic is concerned not only with the individual but with mankind and the cosmos. From this angle the concentration of traditional theology on the individual becomes dubious. But it is still a pity that he does not follow up the approach suggested in these paragraphs. Perhaps it would have helped to overcome the abstract contradiction which he establishes as being present between the hoped-for eschatological reality and the reality of history. In the interests of his inclination towards a revolutionary ideology, Moltmann in the end tears salvation and creation apart, which is neither apocalyptic nor reasonable.

It is extraordinarily instructive to compare Moltmann's reception of apocalyptic with Pannenberg's. For the appeal of the two to the same historical basis is inevitably divergent because of their dependence on very different interpretations. Where the one scents revolution - which is to say rupture and discontinuity - for the other evolution, that is, progress and continuity, seems to be the guiding aim. Thus what is contradictory and 'half-baked' in historical research takes its revenge in the systematic field. Perhaps these dogmatic consequences will one day finally make the historians look rather more closely at their material and produce more reliable results.

Gerhard Sauter's *Zukunft und Verheissung* is the third systematic outline which has copious references to apocalyptic. Sauter wants to show that theological statements are bound to be related to the future. He therefore criticizes in detail modern theology's categorical 'exclusion of apocalyptic', which is largely to be explained as part of an attempt to dissociate theology from an allegedly apocalyptic world picture. What apocalyptic really offers, however, is not a world picture but a 'picture as anticipation of the future which brings every merely fixed "world" into movement'.[27] This, however, is practically the meaningful reacceptance of prophecy, which - as Plöger showed (see above) - came into conflict as inevitably as later apocalyptic with a fixed 'ecclesiastical' society.

> All acceptance of prophetic theology which is not mere academic theory - every acceptance, that is to say, which is a productive continuation, which goes on interpreting prophecy in the light of the claim made by the promise and not under the insignia of fulfilment, inevitably comes into conflict with the theology of a church which is in process of establishing itself, and which can understand the future only as the preservation and extension . . . of its existence.[28]

Sauter's 'yes' to apocalyptic is a limited one, however; he has far greater reservations than Moltmann, let alone Pannenberg. Ultimately God's revelation is promise and not revelation in the sense of *apokalypsis*.[29] According to the Christian witness, man ought not to give himself up to history, either as destiny or as compulsion to self-fulfilment; he ought to hope, within history, for the divine future.[30] Faith needs pictures and metaphors; but only in order that it may thereby be open for an 'incalculable' divine future.[31] From this angle apocalyptic appears as

> the attempt in the light of the future promise to pursue theology in 'eschatological self-containment' - a contradiction in itself, which can show us how a systematic definition is capable of sweeping people off their feet and can lead them astray.[32]

The systematic ventures of these three dogmatic scholars are by no means representative of German and Swiss systematic theology; they are the expressions of a minority, at least in so far as they relate to apocalyptic. There can be no question of apocalyptic literature's having broken through into the systematic theology of our time in any general sense. The latest Protestant dogmatics of W. Trillhaas[33] or the popular Catholic account of J. Ratzinger, *Einführung in das Christentum* (1968), are much more typical of university theology in Germany; and there eschatology plays only a small part and apocalyptic none at all.

The three attempts we have considered recede still further into the background as soon as one devotes any attention at all to the present concern about Christian doctrine in the ecumenical sphere. Apocalyptic ideas - if people are conscious of them as being apocalyptic - play no part whatsoever for dogmatic theologians, students of ethics, or philosophers of religion outside the German-speaking countries.

To illustrate what I mean let us take a brief look at *America*. Following the second General Assembly of the World Council of Churches in Evanston in 1959, which met under the theme 'Christ, the Hope of the World', Neill Q. Hamilton gave a survey called 'The Last Things in the Last Decade'.[34] The article reflects the complete lack of enthusiasm with which American theologians have approached the theme of 'the Christian hope'. This went to such lengths that during the preparations for the conference a famous American theologian declared 'that eschatology had absolutely no significance for him'.[35] What is reavealing for our context is that here the American mood appeals to biblical scholarship and its usual disparaging treatment of the post-exilic period in Israel.

> We are tempted to think that eschatology is a symptom of desperation, a grasping at straws, the figment of a fevered theological imagination. Thus the observation that the doctrine of the two ages (with its disparagement of this world and expectation of a new one) arose after the exile and became generally accepted in Judaism during Maccabean unrest and Roman domination is often taken as proof of such doctrine's invalidity. Judaism went eschatological when it went desperate, and it has been so ever since.[36]

Hamilton himself attempts to dissociate himself from this trend. He seeks a 'personally satisfying, biblically faithful, and socially responsible eschatology',[37] without which the church cannot get along in the long run. For this, it seems to him necessary to distinguish more sharply between eschatology and apocalyptic than has been the general practice in America. Does this mean that American theology is moving towards the line followed by German and Swiss theologians between the two World Wars? It is perhaps not without significance that Hamilton particularly recommends American theologians to read Cullmann.[38]

APOCALYPTIC AS A DISQUIETING MOTIF IN NON-THEOLOGICAL THINKING

1. Apocalyptic images in art and literature

Except for Daniel and Revelation, to whose context no one draws attention, the apocalyptic writings are inaccessible to those of our contemporaries who have no theological training. Consequently the apocalyptic books are less familiar today than the epic of Gilgamesh or ancient Egyptian love songs. Yet the catastrophes which the two World Wars brought in their train have here and there in Europe awakened interest in the book of Revelation; indeed this interest often goes further than theologians and churchmen find quite canny. With the help of apocalyptic images, poets and painters express their despair over the dark side of life. It would be beyond our scope to follow up the details. As a rule in this context apocalyptic is interpreted superficially, as the quintessence of all that is horrible, and as the emotional expression of the end of the world. But there are also those who have concerned themselves more intensively with the themes of apocalyptic history.

The outstanding work of art in this respect is undoubtedly the giant *L'Apocalypse*,[1] This work is a translation of the book of Revelation into seven languages, 'with 21 original paintings on vellum, representing the different styles of contemporary painting' by Bernard Buffet, Salvadore Dali, Leonor Fini, Foujita, Mathieu, Tremois and Zadkine. Interwoven with these are 'poems, observations and meditations on the book of Revelation and its interest for the atomic age' by E.M. Cioran, Jean Cocteau, Daniel Rops, Jean Giono, Jean Guitton, Ernst Jünger and Jean Rostand. Ridiculous though it would be to ignore the commercial character of the undertaking, yet the number of famous names and the choice of this particular book of the Bible shows how the attention of a wide group can be attracted today by the apocalyptic theme.

An extract from Ernst Jünger's contribution, 'Fassungen', may be quoted as an example of the way in which apocalyptic presents itself today:

> Earth will put on a new dress
> as it has put on many before.
> The main thing now is to interpret the signs aright:
> man needs new seismographs,
> - indeed new senses and new observatories.
> His eye is still the instrument of instruments,
> his hand is still the tool of tools.
>
> Deeper than any telescope, further than
> a ray of light, the seer's eye penetrates the world.
> It reaches to the place where beginning and end meet
> and where the pointer falls . . .
> In these visions the universe unveils itself,
> revealing its spirit to the seer.[2]

2. The historical nature of human existence in the context of modern philosophy's historical enquiry

Whatever one may think of the apocalyptic writings, they are at least the documents of an extremely curious way of thinking. But German philosophy, sworn of old to the narrow paths of an esoteric scholastic tradition, has up to now shunned works which breathe anything but the clarity of a timeless and logical terminology. If the signs are not deceptive, however, orthodox philosophy in Germany is beginning to be an even more dubious affair than its theological counterpart at present. So there is a certain fascination in noticing how apocalyptic and its ideas have cropped up on the fringe of philosophical reflection for about the last thirty years. Historical apocalyptic is still only mentioned sporadically in philosophical writings, even more seldom than in systematic theology. But where it is mentioned at all even the philosophers cannot avoid being strongly for or against it.

The end of the First World War, and the breakdown of an optimistic faith in progress, enormously increased the demand in Germany, not only for systematic theology, but also for philosophy - a philosophy which would supply the bearings of existence in the face of an apparently meaningless world. Before the First World War German philosophy was largely concerned with methodological questions belonging to the conflict between science and the arts, and was searching for a clarification of terminological categories in neo-Kantianism; but now the search was for a philosophy which would comprehend man in the tension between inauthentic and authentic existence and which would give him courage for the venture of a decision in which the individual self would be realized precisely through the transcending of all scholarly reflection and all side-stepping arguments. Men like Karl Jaspers and Martin Heidegger were representatives of a philosophy of existence, conceived in these terms, in the 1920s. The cleavage between philosophy and all individual disciplines is stressed. Philosophy of this kind finds itself in unsuspected proximity to theology, whether it likes to admit it or not. It has to come to terms with Christianity in a way which has little in common with the usual nineteenth-century philosophical criticism of religion. How far is Christianity understood historically here, and how far are its eventual apocalyptic features considered?

All his life Heidegger evaded coming to grips with the language of the Christian faith and with theological thinking. That he was able to do so was only possible because of his years in Marburg and his co-operation with the New Testament scholar Bultmann who, along the lines of dialectical theology, called his attention to the distinction between the a-historical kerygma, which springs from divine revelation, and all philosophical and religious history within the world. For Heidegger, what followed from this was the strict divorce between reason and faith, only reason belonging to the sphere with which the philosopher has to concern himself. There are many theologians who regret today that Bultmann was so involved with Heidegger's philosophy in his theology. But perhaps philosophers would have just as much right to complain that Heidegger got too involved philosophically with theology! At all events, Heidegger distinguishes as a matter of course between Christendom as a historical, worldly and political phenomenon (to which he ascribes no great importance) and the Christianity of the New Testament faith.[3] He divides the two so completely that in spite of all his struggles with the history of metaphysics in the last two and a half millennia, historical Christianity in its effect on the history of thought never enters his orbit. All the more, consequently, does apocalyptic as a philosophical theme elude him.

Jaspers, on the other hand, understands the philosophical attitude as a kind of faith and therefore sees himself as being essentially close to biblical religion, about which he is very ready to talk. Biblical religion already contains the idea of the surrounding transcendence; it awakens consciousness of the historical nature of man; and good and evil are comprehended in an absolute either - or. All these are ideas without which philosophy cannot get along. But biblical religion is for Jaspers ultimately determined by the prophets, not first of all by Jesus, let alone by any apocalyptist. Thus he is able to define even the ethical viewpoint as follows: 'Since the days of the prophets, charity is enjoined, culminating in the maxim: "Love thy neighbour as thyself." '[4] Jaspers has expounded his view of human history in *The Origin and Goal of History*. According to this, the period of the prophets (i.e., the period between 800 and 200 BC) is the 'axial period' of human history in general. Together with the contemporary movements in China, India, Iran and Greece, the prophets then formed the basic categories of our present thinking, and for the first time man 'experiences absoluteness in the depths of selfhood and in the lucidity of transcendence'.[5] Jaspers therefore lets the 'axis' period end at the very point where, in the historical view, apocalyptic begins. He is undoubtedly determined in this by theological authorities, who cling tenaciously to the theory of the prophetic connection - who, that is to say, by leaping over five hundred years of Israelite religious history, place Jesus immediately after Deutero-Isaiah. It is only in this light that we can understand why Jaspers sees the picture of world history as a whole as developing in three stages: *(a)* In the mythical theogonies and cosmogonies of earlier peoples; *(b)* In the picture of a divine action reflected in political decisions of will; this is found in the visions of the prophets; and lastly *(c)* in Augustine's conception of one coherent revelatory event, stretching from the creation of the world to its end.[6] Jaspers has never noticed that the third stage, at least, was already reached in the apocalyptic writings - and no theologian has ever told him. What is totally absent in Jaspers, and what makes it easy for him to pass over apocalyptic, is any regard at all for the eschatological themes of 'biblical religion'.

Wilhelm Kamlah's *Christentum und Selbstbehauptung*[7] also belongs to the existentialist orbit but it has a sounder historical foundation. Here Kamlah also takes issue with Jaspers. This is the first time that apocalyptic assumes an important position in philosophical reasoning.

Kamlah's starting point is the recognition that the philosophical talk about historicality as the authentic essence of man makes it necessary for us to enquire where historically existing man is to be found and how long he has existed. Philosophy cannot dispense with a further question to history about man; for it has to watch for 'the break through of man's potentiality for being man, over and above his purely biological genesis'. Here, however, all that is available to us is western tradition, which is all that we understand and which therefore possesses authority for us.[8] It takes us back to two roots, the Greek and the Christian, the latter being decisive for our present theme. Kamlah tries to interpret Jesus (or rather the founding era of Christianity down to Augustine) as the axis of world history, because it is in this period that the historical attitude was formed for the first time. For it was now that the world was radically secularized, and in this way man was set at a distance from the rest of the world; this, in its turn, then made it possible for him to think 'creatively' in modern times (though this does not mean that Kamlah approves of the modern way of thinking).[9]

This attitude was prepared for by Israelite historicality, but only prepared. Here the prophets played a determining role by proclaiming the impotence of all earthly kingdoms, by renouncing, in true historicality, political self-assertion and by waiting only for the kingdom of God. But the prophets were not the final stage before the rise of Christianity. Jaspers' theory of the prophetic connection is expressly repudiated.[10] For the prophets still see in the kingdom of God 'a new order in the community of peoples: the oppression of the poor and of widows and orphans will come to an end'.[11] It is the apocalyptists who go a step further. With their doctrine of the two ages they make creation part of Jewish historicality. This development finds its crowning in Jesus; for with Jesus the eschatological future no longer has anything to do with any longings for self-assertion, and is in fact no longer a temporal future at all. The same thing is true with Paul:

> Christ is not the turn of the age in the sense that with him a new historical world begins; he is so in that the hearers of the kerygma are to be converted and receive salvation *now*: 'Now is the day of salvation.'[12]

This Christian experience of the eschatological abolition of history allows the paradox of human historicality to become evident in the most radical way. 'History means: things cannot remain as they are; and yet things are again and again what they cannot remain.'[13] Historicality becomes for us simply a truth which affects us all, that every one of us in his own situation is to experience human individuality and self-assertion.[14]

Kamlah's book is illuminating. It shows on the one hand how the existentialist view of human existence forces us to further historical questions, which inevitably lead beyond the canon of an 'orthodox' history of philosophy (Plato, Descartes, Kant) and which raises Christianity to a philosophical problem. Kamlah takes precedence of Jaspers in his perception of the continuous eschatological tendency of biblical religion. In this way apocalyptic becomes a logical part of things. Yet his outline remains ultimately unhistorical because for him man's 'becoming' man really ends with primitive Christianity (or with Augustine); with which the present is directly linked. In order to make this leap possible it is really necessary to depict Christianity in modernistic terms. The transition from apocalyptic to primitive Christianity is depicted in a way which is dangerous for Kamlah's concept - namely that with a renunciation of the demythologizing, modernistic inter-pretation, Jesus and Paul immediately slip back to the stage of pre-Christian apocalyptic - as soon, that is to say, as the temporal statements of the two about the divine future are taken literally! That Kamlah does not perceive these dangerous shoals is due to the influence of his teacher Bultmann, and probably above all to his authorities K.G. Kuhn and Vielhauer who, according to his epilogue, gave him 'their disinterested advice out of their supreme knowledge of the subject'.[15]

Another work to be written in the shadow of Marburg and Heidegger, though displaying much sharper opposition to its origin, is Karl Löwith's *Meaning in History.*[16] This book too concerns itself philosophically with the meaning of Christianity for contemporary man and, like Kamlah, ascribes great importance to the eschatological theme, although apocalyptic is admittedly passed over. Not only is Löwith's sceptical position remote from existentialism; it repudiates all talk about history as a basic category of human existence, whether this theory appears in Marxist or historical form. Perhaps it is not by chance that the book originated in America.[17] In Germany such aloofness from historical determinism would probably have been harder of conception. Be that as it may, in his investigation of what he considers the excessive over-valuation of history, Löwith arrives at Christianity as being the real cause. All speculations about the philosophy of history, down to Hegel and Marx, ultimately derive from Christian influence. Yet Christianity has not simply striven towards a grasp of political world history. On the contrary, in its original form it aims at a salvation history which is far removed from, and irreconcilable with, secular history. But from the very beginning Christians looked for the future consummation of world time and in the course of the history of thought this attitude was transferred to secular history. If what is said about Christianity in its original form is correct, the Old Testament Jewish view of history (and consequently apocalyptic as well) cannot have been the foundation of Christianity. Rather,

> The only antagonism which is not accidental, but intrinsic to the message of the New Testament, is the antagonism to Jewish futurism (expecting the Messiah in the future instead of recognizing him in the presence of Jesus) and to the apocalyptic *calculations* of the last events by Jews as well as by Christians.[18]

This sentence shows how strongly Löwith is still influenced by his former teacher Bultmann, in spite of his (justifiable) criticism of the way in which Bultmann and Heidegger attempt to interpret the temporal futurism of the New Testament faith.[19] But Löwith adheres to the anti-apocalyptic interpretation of primitive Christianity and its eschatology as a matter of course.[20]

3. Philosophy under the influence of sociological questionings

Since 1960 the importance of sociological questioning has been growing in all disciplines. Above all, however, the form of sociology which is directed towards the criticism of ideologies and the alteration of existing conditions has deeply influenced student opposition in western Europe. Whether it is the Utopian exuberance of youth or the nightmare of the older beneficiaries of the affluent society, the word 'apocalyptic' plays so great a part in radio and press in connection with student demands and actions that it would repay an investigation of its own. Apocalyptic is one of the few theological terms which has been absorbed into the jargon of the mass media.[21]

More important in our context, where our concern is a scholarly one, are the *philosophical* attempts to set the processes of society in which mankind finds itself within a wider historical framework. It is true that the range seldom extends beyond the beginnings of the modern period. History before the Enlightenment and the industrial revolution becomes for sociologists and philosophers frequently uninteresting and oddly homogeneous - homogeneous in its unimportance. This is also true where it is (neo-) Marxist influences which prevail. Thus conditions before modern times were for Jürgen Habermas, for example, stamped for thousands of years by the advanced civilizations.

These represent a certain stage in the evolution of the human race. They are distinguished from primitive forms of society: first through the fact of a centralized rule . . .; secondly, through the division of society into socio-economic classes . . .; thirdly, through the fact that some sort of picture of the world (myth, advanced religion) is in force, for the purpose of effectively legitimizing the ruling power.[22]

In view of such a primitive concept of advanced civilization (centralized power and a picture of the world as the opposite pole to modern history) it would of course seem superfluous to look for anything as out-of-the-way as apocalyptic. And yet - in view of the widespread and popular Marxist theory of religion as the legitimation of the ruling power - apocalyptic must actually become a glaring problem. For it would seem that nowhere in literature before modern times is power in all its forms so much open to question and so stripped of virtue as in these very apocalyptic books. But which of the sociologists and their eager supporters cares about that?

At the same time, honourable mention must be made of two exceptions. Two German-speaking philosophers have allotted apocalyptic an important place in the history of ideas, although the place they choose may not convince every reader, least of all the specialist.

In 1966 Hans Blumenberg published his book entitled *Die Legitimät der Neuzeit*. According to this, the modern period was preceded by an era moulded by Christianity. It was ruled for centuries by the one theme of theodicy - the task of justifying God's existence and actions in the face of a wicked world. The modern period brought about a radical breach with this practice. Man finds himself, and decides to put an end to the evils of the world. The breach was inevitable and is irreversible. The central position of theodicy in the preceding period, however, derived largely from pre-Christian *apocalyptic*.

> Jewish apocalyptic . . . compensated for . . . the failure of the historical expectations of a nation by prophesying their fulfilment beyond history, in order thus to justify the God of their people and the nation's history.[23]

Here apocalyptic appears as the foundation not only of primitive Christianity but also of the intellectual history of the west generally, before modern times; although it is admittedly a foundation from which we have finally to dissociate ourselves.

In his recent book *Atheismus im Christentum* Ernst Bloch

finds apocalyptic equally vital for the history for the last two thousand years. But his evaluation is quite different from Blumenberg's. For him apocalyptic is quite simply the revolutionary impulse; it is, that is to say, Christianity's *positive heritage*. Bloch's interpretation is, it is true, accompanied by a fantastic interpretation of the biblical texts which can sometimes distort his undertaking to a ludicrous degree for the critical reader. In the style of the Enlightenment, Bloch believes in the existence of a priestly caste which has distorted and edited the text of the Bible in the interests of the ruling classes. Ezra is a particularly black sheep.[24] The true basis of the Bible, however, is anti-authoritarian - it looks for the overthrow of unjust conditions, confirming the saying that 'wherever there is hope there too is religion'.[25]

The revolutionary impetus is particularly clear in the book of Revelation. Luther, the 'restorer', had good reason for calling the last book of the Bible 'every mob-leader's bag of tricks'.[26] For its eschatology is not an 'interior' one.

It contains the strongest discontent within all *religion,* all ties with the past; what is adventist in it is entirely without *ordo sempiternus rerum.*[27]

But it is only in this light that the figure of Jesus can be interpreted. Biblical criticism, standing in the service of the ruling classes, has completely distorted him.

To such a degree did the men of the Enlightenment and then - less innocently - the anti-Semitic liberal theologians separate Jesus from the Jewish messianic dream - that is to say from the eschatology which is also political. This kind of thing unfortunately began with Renan's *Life of Jesus,* was initiated in the scholarly field by Holtzmann, Wellhausen and Harnack, and ended with a Christ of incomparably pure inwardness'.[28]

In actual truth, however, Jesus' position was quite different and 'his moral teaching is incomprehensible without its apocalyptic content'.[29] The Sermon on the Mount is an ethic for the end of history, for the time following the struggle. But for the present the watchword is: I am come not to send peace but a sword.

Objectively what Jesus did least of all was to skulk in 'inwardness' and withdrawal; nor did he behave as if he were billeting officer for a completely transcendent kingdom of heaven.[30]

On the contrary: a direct line can be drawn from the apocalyptic Jesus, not only to Thomas Müntzer but even to the French revolution of 1789, which William Blake once rightly hailed:

But terrible Orc, when he beheld the morning in the east,
Shot from the heights of Enitharmon,
And in the vineyards of red France appear'd the light of his fury.[31]

There is not much point in criticizing these ideas from the angle of historical apocalyptic. But do not such utterances show how the imprecise and tendentious way in which many commentators form their precipitate judgments of apocalyptic is reflected outside biblical scholarship and, inevitably, in exaggerated and coarser form? This is the revenge for theology's inadequate investigations of the history of our world and the early history of Christianity.

WHY THINGS MUST CHANGE: A HIGHLY SUBJECTIVE EPILOGUE

Talk is rife among younger theologians today to the effect that historical-critical research into the Bible is finished with, essentially speaking. If any proof were needed of how foolish this judgment is, it is provided by a look at the study of apocalyptic. What is written about apocalyptic today usually culminates in the flinging down of swift wholesale judgments, which closer inspection shows go back to the secondary literature of the era before the First World War, when scholars were using methods of research which have long since become antiquated. It is hard to detect any study of the primary texts, at least in continental theology. Yet there is sufficient material at our disposal, and better methods have long been available for acquiring well-founded information about what apocalyptic was. These methods are scarely ever employed, however. If this state of affairs continues, German biblical scholarship will soon lose its reputation for historical integrity and reliability - the reputation of which it was once so proud.

But the point at issue is in truth more than the reputation of a single discipline. What we have already discovered in our quick (all too quick!) run through of the theology and philosophy of our time gives rise to the suspicion that decisive aspects of theology in general (perhaps even of philosophy and sociology) are connected with the attitude of leading scholars to the curious by-ways which we have been considering. Why has research into the apocalyptic writings declined? How can this be remedied? One reason for the decline is undoubtedly the insufficient application to these writings of otherwise approved historical methods - we have only to think of form criticism. But why is methodological accuracy - so much striven for in exegetical disciplines - neglected here? In order to answer these questions, we shall be bound to go beyond the sphere of specialist apocalyptic research.

In what follows I am for the most part speaking dogmatically. My primary aim is to provoke - to rouse others to different and better explanations. I shall confine myself to two main subjects because I suspect that it is here that we can find the reasons why the range of the questions which commentators ask in their treatment of the apocalypses is so curiously limited.

1. Kerygma and canon

From a superficial point of view the attitude of biblical scholars (and the people who quote them) towards apocalyptic literature can be explained by the increasing *specialization* of Old and New Testament studies. It is not as if the state of exegetical research, as regards work on individual Old and New Testament books, were a lamentable one in general. Anyone of discernment is bound to respect the remarkable degree of penetration which is employed in the illumination of philological, terminological and form-critical problems in the individual biblical writings. There is probably no field of philology or history in general in which every iota in the documents is so carefully examined as in the exegesis of the Bible. Nor can it be generally maintained that the commentators ignore the non-biblical world. The recently discovered Dead Sea Scrolls, for example, have been studied by many biblical scholars. A quantity of extra-biblical material, and especially archeological discoveries, is being gathered together for the illumination of the biblical text.

Yet it is at this point that the weakness of present biblical scholarship becomes evident. The non-biblical material which is used is employed in a purely illustrative way; its exegetical application seems superficial and a matter of chance; the material is not fitted together with the biblical statements into one overall context of life, since it is not understood as being the product of one and the same history. But not only is the connection of the late biblical period with the conditions of

Hellenistic and Roman society neglected; the connection between the Old and New Testaments is no longer ever presented as a stirring and forward-striving history of hope and action, of believing and speaking, of suffering and conquering. The commentators of today shun the imputation of producing a historical reconstruction like the plague. But to investigate history does in fact mean reconstruction; and anyone who does not like it will never arrive at a result which will stand up to inspection.

Having avoided the Scylla of possible speculative reconstructions, the commentators promptly land in the Charybdis of an anachronistic equating of the 'situation' of each individual 'text' with the 'situation' of 'man today', the two allegedly coinciding. The anachronism is shamefacedly masked by the term 'kerygma' which is supposed to emphasize the point that the Word of God is valid today in exactly the same way as it was in the past. But the difference between what man was in ancient times and what he is in essence today, grows in proportion to the progress of historical research. It is no wonder that theological exegesis is becoming more and more colourless and anaemic.

It is true that theology - even historical theology - always has to do in a decisive sense with words and language. But the modern term 'kerygma' (which is by no means identical with the Pauline concept) is gradually obscuring more than it illuminates. Where people are looking for kerygma, they inevitably remain within the narrow walls of the church's received Old and New Testament *canon*. It is true that the earlier notion of the canon, which was coupled with the doctrine of inspiration, has long become suspect. The biblical texts are ostensibly interpreted according to the same methods as other ancient documents. But no theologian, as far as I know, has yet tried to trace the kerygma of a non-biblical gnostic or apocalyptic text! The modern dogmatic term 'kerygma' narrows down from the outset the material which would seem to repay the effort of intensive historical investigation, restricting it to the field of the traditional canon - even in places where within these writings scholars are still seeking for a canon within the canon.

The conscious or unconscious narrowing down of serious

biblical scholarship to kerygma and canon involves the danger that what the Bible says about God will no longer be understood in the light of the full context of life as lived at the time. What is written about apocalyptic presents us with melancholy examples. But where the total context of the life of the time is unrecognized, what the Bible can mean today will not be sufficiently evident either. Will the increasing specialization of Old and New Testament exegesis, theologically upheld by the ideas of kerygma and canon, not in the long run make this exegesis completely sterile for present-day theology and preaching? Apocalyptic research, at least, threatens to perish completely as a result of the trend.

2. The unique character of the Christian faith

It would be a cheap way out to let matters rest with the mere reproach that many Old and New Testament scholars are historical or philological specialists influenced by a superseded notion of the canon and seeing their theological responsibility at most in the extraction of a kerygma out of a mass of detail. There are a whole number of theologians who consider seriously why they work so intensively on the biblical texts in particular. It is true that the search for a Christian absolute, which so much tormented the nineteenth century, has been abandoned as not being to the purpose. But what makes the Christian faith unique compared with other human attitudes of mind is a question which is still asked again and again, and the answer is largely derived from the Bible - whether by referring to the divine revelation in law and gospel; or to the justification of the ungodly; or to man's newly revealed self-understanding; or even to the freedom of speech which Christ conferred for the very first time. These solutions, all of which have been proposed in turn by exegetical and systematic theologians, ascertain the unique character of the Christian faith phenomenologically out of a particular experience of the present, trying to verify this, more or less as an afterthought, from the biblical texts. There is no objection to this procedure if it is joined with the necessary readiness to correct the theory as soon as the historical texts lay their embargo upon it.

This readiness seems to be lacking, however, as soon as the

borderline of the traditional canon has to be crossed. This applies not least to the sideways glance which scholars give at pre-Christian apocalyptic. The passion with which judgments for and against the apocalypses are expressed today is suspicious. It cannot be explained from the content of the apocalyptic texts, if these are viewed in themselves. The problem of apocalyptic is rather the problem of Jesus, and the problem of Jesus is still the problem of the special character of the Christian faith. Whatever a writer's historical evaluation of the apocalyptic writings turns out to be, our survey has shown that the historical Jesus (and with him, at least since the end of the Second World War, the dogmatic or philosophical Christ as well) always appears in that particular light.

Where apocalyptic is praised - as by Pannenberg or Bloch, for example - Jesus is also interpreted as an apocalyptist; a high regard for apocalyptic in its bearings on the present and on true Christianity heightens the significance of the person and destiny of Jesus. Where little value is placed on apocalyptic, however (as with Ebeling and the New Testament scholars deriving from Bultmann, or among the conservatively minded), it is rejected so decidedly in order that the splendour of the unique character of Jesus as the witness of faith or as the quintessence of the idea of the fellow-man may shine out all the more clearly through the contrast with apocalyptic ideas. Wherever Christian Old Testament scholars treat apocalyptic disparagingly and contrast it with the prophets of the Old Testament canon, they do so in order to show Jesus and the Christian proclamation as the continuation and (typological) transcending of the true Old Testament faith.

What must be done in order to free the majority of theologians from their secret fear that Jesus, or the Christ of the New Testament, may be akin to apocalyptic? The question of the uniqueness of the Christian faith is certainly necessary; but somehow it must be wrongly slanted if (as has been usual hitherto) it is coupled with the postulated uniqueness of the proclamation of Jesus before Easter, or the Christ who was preached afterwards. It is this impression at least which the many embarrassed statements force upon us. But why not deduce the uniqueness of Jesus from the story of his ministry, where it is obvious?

With its talk about an almighty God and his appointed Kyrios, Jesus, Christianity completely snuffed out all the religions of the ancient East and of the Hellenistic and Roman world. Here if anywhere it must be possible to elicit the uniqueness of the Christian faith in such a way that it is in accordance with the historical facts and does not compel us to force historical phenomena into a dogmatic bed of Procrustes. In order to arrive at results in this way, we must of course not only contrast the historical Jesus with his late Israelite and Hellenistic environment; we must, as it were, *link* him organically with the whole life of his time - and why not with the apocalyptists as well? If the saying about the kingdom of Christ not being of this world be understood in the sense that the Christian faith has nothing essentially to do with the history of mankind and the structures of human society (and this is the way in which modern theologians would like it to be understood), then the progress of Christianity in the late ancient world and in the European middle ages, and also in the mission fields of the nineteenth century, makes complete historical nonsense; for this progress showed Christianity to be a unique force in the history of language. Here apocalyptic partly played no role at all; and partly an important one.

Most German-speaking theologians reject with the utmost vigour the idea that the uniqueness of the true, Christian faith can be grounded in the uniqueness of Christianity. Is not Christianity a historical phenomenon and thus a relative power? Is not Christianity even a religion? For the last fifty years German-speaking Protestant theologians have been striving to detach the Christian faith from all religion (at least as an idea) and thus to dissociate it from Christianity as a religious phenomenon as well. These efforts have not been successful up to now and they will be even less so in the future. Associated with them are numerous, usually naive attempts to set up a fundamental wall of partition between the descriptive study of religion and a theology orientated towards faith; and it is these attempts among other things which have led to the confusion which has made the apocalyptic controversy such a hopeless one. In order to achieve the goal of separating faith from religion, theology would have to dispense with historical research. For historical research never proves mere discontinuity; it always shows continuity as well. To abandon historical research, however, today simply means completely renouncing Jesus of Nazareth.

It seems to me that the only way out is to turn the wheel full circle. We must finally grasp that Christianity is a religion, but a religion with a role in religious history which is as necessary as it is unique. Only then will the tendency of the questions framed by the exegetes be so free of bias that they can deal objectively with the connection between the Old Testament prophets and the apocalyptists, and with the relation of Jesus to apocalyptic. Then the connection of the figure of Jesus, as well as the biblical statements surrounding him, with the present day will also become compellingly clear. But this presupposes that the theologians find the courage for a theory of history - and that means for overall historical reconstructions also. Exegetical theology will probably not be able to avoid returning in the future to the history of religion and to a search for general historical patterns, if it still wants to play a role in general theology in the days to come.

Our survey has shown sufficiently that late Israelite and early Christian apocalyptic is not one branch of the literature of the ancient world among many others, a sector which one may consider philologically and exegetically or leave alone, according to taste. Does the apocalyptic world of ideas not represent the change-over between the Testaments, i.e., does it not reflect that religious movement which, under the impression of the person of Jesus and his destiny, permitted a part of late Israel to merge into early Christianity? This question has been in the air for the last hundred years. An adequate answer has not yet been found down to the present day. At the moment there is an additional idea: whether it is not the very heritage which Jesus and the early church took over from apocalyptic (the heritage which so forcibly expresses the futurist trend of faith in God) which, in the face of the desperate situation of systematic theology and philosophy, provides aspects under which theology will again be convincingly possible in the future. At this point too we are still far from convincing solutions.

Everything suggests that in the coming decades theology will have to concern itself increasingly with the apocalyptic writings. *Old Testament scholarship* will not escape, as soon as it traces the history of Yahweh worship and faith up to the point where the Old Testament visibly begins to merge either into the New or into the Talmud. And, unless this extension is made, the use of the Old Testament by Christianity will be unjustifiable in the long run; since the era of the easy theory of the prophetic connection will one day come to an end.

New Testament exegesis will not be able to avoid the theme because the question of the historical Jesus demands a clear and concrete historical answer. We would probably not be wrong in the impression that, if theology wants still to be taken seriously by contemporary man, its christological statements will have to be more precise. But where is this precision to come from if not from historical research?

In the framework of the *history of dogma and theology* apocalyptic *must* be discussed as soon as the question of 'Christianity' as a general force is raised - the question of what the Christian faith has given men in the way of historical consciousness, futurist direction of mind, and principles of conduct. Even *systematic theology* will not be able to avoid a further consideration of the apocalyptic theme. What Pannenberg and Moltmann have presented are certainly individualist theses and theories. But one gets the impression that they are the first signs of the protest of a younger generation. Up to now Protestant theology, whether it set out to be Lutheran or pietistic, liberal, dialectical or personalist, has been all too concerned with the conscience and salvation of the individual soul, with the justification of the individual alone. A new generation of theologians is not able to take itself and the decision of the individual so seriously. It is not content with abstract worldliness, let alone detachment from the world; it presses for social responsibility and the modification of the world. In so far as it is concerned with theology, this generation asks about God's workings in the decisive forces of our time. But here either a past or a future aspect is necessary, according to one's frame of mind, and probably both. This certainly does not mean that God becomes the guarantor of the existing order. God's absence is more noticeable than his presence. But the negative side of human existence is not experienced by our intellectual contemporaries as unalterable 'man' in Heidegger's sense, but as alterable 'manipulation', reducible in the future, in Marcuse's sense.

In the sphere of the biblical writings, accordingly, there is little which is so significant as apocalyptic. True, the apocalyptists do not know anything about the social activity of believers, but they apparently proclaim that the world is constantly being shaped and reshaped by God; they announce a mighty and ultimate divine revolution, and hold up to the eyes of the reader the goal of a renewed human society which has become one with its God and thus with the enduring ground of all reality. Do they not even paint the picture of a society in which the rule of man over man has hence been set aside for ever? The apocalyptists demand that believers, on their own historical plane, 'project' themselves in the direction of this hope. Is this of no importance for our present time?

Through the attempts to grasp anew the obscure power of apocalyptic, a new movement has unmistakably entered theology, a movement which can be salutary if it brings a careful working out and evaluation of the material in its train. If it does not, great will be the harm among theologians and non-theologians alike.

NOTES

CHAPTER II

1. *Die Apokryphen und Pseudepigraphen des Alten Testaments,* übersetzt und herausgegeben von E. Kautzsch, 1900, 1921[2], 1962[3].

2. Reissued as *Die Eschatologie der jüdischen Gemeinde im neutestamentlichen Zeitalter,* 1934,[2] 1966[3].

3. Revised by H. Gressmann as *Die Religion des Judentums im späthellenistischen Zeitalter,* 1926[3], 1966[4] (with foreword by E. Lohse).

4. The non-canonical New Testament apocalypses were made available by E. Hennecke in *Neutestamentliche Apokryphen in deutscher Übersetzung,* 1904, 1924[2]; revised by W. Schneemelcher *et al.,* 1959-64,[3] the apocalyptic texts in Vol. II introduced by P. Vielhauer. ET ed.by R. McL. Wilson, *New Testament Apocrypha* I-II, 1963-65. As far as I am aware, no comprehensive account of New Testament and early Christian apocalyptic has yet been attempted.

5. 'Die Anfänge christlicher Theologie', *ZTK* 57, 1960, pp. 162-85; reprinted in *Exegetische Versuche und Besinnungen* II, 1965[2], pp. 82-104; ET, 'The Beginnings of Christian Theology', in *New Testament Questions of Today,* 1969, pp. 82-107; citation from p. 180=100; ET, p. 102.

6. In 'Heilsgeschehen und Geschichte', *KuD* 5, 1959, pp. 218-37, 259-88; reprinted in *Grundfragen systematischer Theologie,* 1967, pp. 22-78; ET, 'Redemptive Event and History', *Basic Questions in Theology,* 1970, pp. 15-80.

CHAPTER III

1. The *Neue Brockhaus* of 1964, vol. 1, p.96, defines the German word 'apokalyptisch' as 'geheimnisvoll, dunkel', i.e., 'mysterious, obscure', and so does the *Brockhaus Enzyklopädie,* 1966, I, p.612. The OED, on the other hand, with its definition 'of the nature of revelation or disclosure', ignores these associations.

2. G. Sauter, *Zukunft und Verheissung,* 1965, p.95, cf. p.229.

3. O. Cullmann, *Heil als Geschichte,* 1965, p.62; ET, *Salvation in History,* 1967, p.80.

4. For example the leading Jewish religious philosopher Martin Buber, cf. Freiherr von Hammerstein, 'Das Messiasproblem bei M. Buber', *Studia Delitzschiana* 1, 1958, pp. 23-25. A remarkable swing is taking place at present in American Judaism, however. In his foreword to the Dropsie College edition of Jewish Apocryphal Literature (in the first work to appear, S. Tedesche and S. Zeitlin, *The First Book of Maccabees,* 1950,

pp. Xf.), Abraham Neuman writes that Enoch and IV Ezra reveal the spirit of the Jewish martyrs better than the writings of Josephus. The apocalyptic books are certainly nearer to the New Testament than to (late) Jewish literature. But nevertheless 'we deem it an act of redemption to reclaim these works for the Jewish people and to restore them to their rightful place of honor in Jewish literature.'

5. Hennecke-Schneemelcher II, p. 408 (ET,p.582); E. Lohmeyer, *Die Offenbarung des Johannes,* 2nd ed. by H. Kraft (HNT 16), 1953, on 1.1.

6. Survey in J.E. Ménard, 'Les manuscrits de Nag Hammadi', *Bibliotheca Orientalis* 13, 1956, pp. 2-6, and in S. Schulz, *TR* 26, 1960, pp. 237-50.

7. Survey in O. Eissfeldt, *Einleitung in das Alte Testament,* 1964[3](ET, *The Old Testament: an Introduction,*1965), section 110; C. Burchard, *Bibliographie zu den Handschriften vom Toten Meer* II (BZAW 89), 1965, pp. 333-6.

8. P. Feine and J. Behm, *Einleitung in das Neue Testament,* 14th ed. by W.G. Kümmel, 1965 (ET, *Introduction to the New Testament,* 1966), section 33.

9. D.S. Russell, *The Method and Message of Jewish Apocalyptic,* 1964, p.28; G. von Rad, *Theologie des Alten Testaments II,* 1965[4], p.327.

10. Eissfeldt, *op. cit.,* p.711 (ET,p.524); Kutscher, *Scripta Hierosolymitana* 4,1958,2. Russell contemplates people who reached Palestine from Mesopotamia during the Maccabean rebellion, *op.cit.,* p.19.

11. At present vigorously supported by F. M. Cross: 'That which places a gulf between the Essenes and the main stream of Judaism is their apocalypticism . . . In no case can the Pharisees, much less the Sadducees, be called apocalyptists.' *The Ancient Library of Qumran,* 1958, p.54 n.33; cf. also B. Reicke in *JBL* 79, 1960, pp. 137-50.

12. 'The Apocalyptic literature and the Zealot Movement went hand in hand, the one providing the dangerous food and the other feasting on it and calling for more.' R.T. Herford, *The Pharisees,* 1924, p.188.

13. Cf. also von Rad in the first ed. of his *Theologie des Alten Testament* II, 1960, p.314; ET of first ed., *Old Testament Theology* II, 1965, pp. 301f.

14. My book *Was ist Formgeschichte?,* 1967[2] (ET, *The Growth of the Biblical Tradition,* 1969) explains in detail why the approach offered by form criticism and literary history plays a decisive part for biblical and related writings (i.e., not only for the apocalypses). I can therefore confine myself here to a few key points.

15. The view taken by A. Nissen in 'Tora und Geschichte in Spätjudentum', *NovT* X, 1967, p.246 (without detailed evidence); and by von Rad in *Theologie* II, 1965[4], p.330 n.28.

16. On II Baruch and IV Ezra cf. B. Violet, *Die Apokalypsen des Esra und des Baruch in deutscher Gestalt* (GCS), 1924.

17. Cf. also Rev. 5.1; Dan. 7.2; II Bar. 36.2f.; IV Ezra 13.2; I Enoch 90.1f., cf.1.2; Apocalypse of Abraham 21.2; and in the prophetic writings Ezek.1.4; Zech.1.8; and frequently elsewhere. If an actual vision has been described, the transition to the second, interpretative section is marked

by the words: 'This was the vision (word, dream) . . . and its interpretation is . . .' (Dan.2.36; 4.18; IV Ezra 10.40-43, cf. 12.10; II Bar.39.1f.).

18. Rev. 1.17; 4.2; Dan.10; II Bar. 21.26; IV Ezra 5.14; I Enoch 65.4; Apoc. Abraham 10.2.

19. Whether the paraenetic (component) literary types have any close connection with the popularity of Wisdom discourses in the late Israelite period, or with the turning of post-exilic prophecy to hortatory discourses (Trito-Isaiah, Malachi) has not yet been clarified. The part played by ethics in the apocalypses cannot be too highly estimated. 'Apocalyptic was essentially ethical' (Charles, *Apocrypha and Pseudepigrapha of the Old Testament*, 1913,II,p.ix).

20. On the legends in the early parts of the Old Testament see *Was ist Formgeschichte?* (ET, *Growth* . . .), section 16.

21. British and American scholars particularly have offered various explanations: (1) The absolute validity of the Law and the period staked out by the canon no longer allowed of contemporary prophecy (Charles, *Apocrypha* II, p.viii). (2) The author is falling back on a long oral tradition which circulated under the name in question (W.O.E. Oesterley, *The Jews and Judaism during the Greek Period*, 1941, p.74). (3) The dominating factor is the peculiar Hebrew concept of an 'extension of personality' (D.S. Russell, *Between the Testaments*, 1959,p.116; cf. also *The Method and Message of Jewish Apocalyptic*, 1964, pp. 127-39). In Germany the old 'deception' hypothesis is also still in vogue. According to this the apocalyptic writers, though knowing better, deliberately had recourse to a fiction in order to lend credibility to their writings (cf. von Rad, *Theologie des Alten Testaments* II,[4] p.320). English-speaking scholars dissociate themselves from this suspicion: 'It is improbable that (the pseudonymity) deceived anyone, or was intended to' (H.H. Rowley, *The Relevance of Apocalyptic*, 1944, p.14). H.R. Balz's essay, 'Anonymität und Pseudonymität in Urchristentum' (*ZTK* 66, 1969, pp.403-36), though full of useful material, is typical of the German attitude, with its remoteness from all the deeper problems. He finds Russell's thesis weighed down by 'a whole series of prior judgments' (n.39). He evidently imagines his own solution to be free of all such judgments. The answer he proposes for the book of Daniel is as follows: 'If the author had written under his own name, however, he would no doubt have met with incredulity on the part of his contemporaries, for his visionary accounts are not descriptions of actual experiences; they are conscious literary inventions' (p.422). Balz unfortunately fails to reveal the source of his information.

22. Rev. 13; Dan. 7; II Bar. 36f.; IV Ezra 11; I Enoch 85ff.; Apoc. Abr. 13. Von Rad (*Theologie* II[4], p.319) sees, however, in the 'rational character of apocalyptic . . . the exact opposite of every kind of genuine mythological thinking.'

23. Rev. 5; II Bar. 35ff.; 53ff.; IV Ezra 12. The symbols of redemption are generally taken from Old Testament prophecy.

24. For further explanation see my *Was ist Formgeschichte?* (ET, *Growth* . . .), section 2D.

25. See *Was ist Formgeschichte?*, p.5 (ET,pp.4f.).
26. Rev. 20.6f.; Dan.9; II Bar. 27; IV Ezra 7.28; I Enoch 85ff., 93; Apoc. Abr. 29.
27. Dan. 10.20f.; I Enoch 89.59ff, cf. Rev. 16.14; Apoc. Abr. 10.17.
28. Rev. 21.12; Dan. 12.3; I Enoch 51.4; II Bar. 51.5; IV Ezra 7.97.
29. Rev. 20.4-6; Dan.12; II Bar. 50f.; IV Ezra 7.32; I Enoch 22; 51.
30. Rev. 21; II Bar. 6.8f.; IV Ezra 8.52-54; I Enoch 48f.; Apoc. Abr. 29.17.
31. Rev. 20.11; Dan. 7.19; II Bar. 73.1; IV Ezra 7.33; Apoc. Abr. 18.
32. Cf. my essay, 'Der Schatz im Himmel', in *Leben jenseits des Todes, Festschrift für H. Thielicke*, 1968, pp. 47-60.
33. Scholars occasionally question whether a human or angelic mediator is an essential figure in apocalyptic eschatology, maintaining that the dominating feature is a *theocratic* view, according to which God alone brings about final redemption. Murdock (*Interpretation* 21, 1967, p.175 n.29) cites I Enoch 16; 71f.; 91; II Enoch 33; 50.2 B; 65f.; Ass. Moses 9-10.6 as examples of 'the expectation of the "future aeon" without a messianic kingdom on earth.' The discrepancy is most clearly emphasized by P. Vielhauer ('Gottesreich und Menschensohn in der Verkündigung Jesu' in *Festschrift G. Dehn*, 1957, pp. 51-79; reprinted in *Aufsätze zum Neuen Testament*, 1965, pp. 55-91; 'Jesus und der Menschensohn', *ZTK* 60, 1963, pp. 133-77, reprinted in *Aufsätze* pp.92-140). Where the eschatological future is expected and designated as the rule of God, the Son of man is missing; 'but in this case the Messiah, or any other judge-saviour figure, is missing as well' (*ZTK*, p.135). Vielhauer cites the Similitudes of Enoch and IV Ezra for the Son of man as essential mediator, but he excludes Dan.7 because there the Messiah is not an individual figure. For the sovereignty which relates to God alone he quotes Dan.2; Sibylline Oracles II 767; Assumption of Moses 10.1ff.
Because this point is much discussed in connection with a noticeable relationship between apocalyptic and New Testament writings a few observations may perhaps not be out of place:
1. Of all the many interpretations of the well-worn passage in Dan.7, the one suggested by Vielhauer is surely the most improbable; for according to 7.14 the Son of man of 7.13 (who, Vielhauer tells us, is a symbolic figure representing the eschatological kingdom) receives that very same eternal sovereignty and everlasting kingdom which are God's alone according to 3.33. According to Vielhauer, therefore, the symbol (Son of man=eschatological kingdom) has to 'receive' the very thing (i.e., the kingdom) which it itself is initiating. What is this supposed to mean?
2. For Enoch a reference to 41.1, compared with 61.8; 69.26-29 and the throne concept in general, is enough to shake the theory of an unrelated parallelism between the rule of God and the figure of the mediator.
3. IV Ezra 13 certainly does not expressly mention the rule of God, but the (Son of) man cuts out for himself a great mountain (v.6) and flies up upon it, which is undoubtedly a reference to Dan. 2.34,44,

where the stone which frees itself is expressly related to 'the kingdom'.

4. What is said in Dan. 2.34f., 44f, is interpreted by Vielhauer as referring to an absolutely established kingdom of God, without any human representatives. But Daniel talks about a new, fifth empire, which replaces the empires of the world which are ruled over by kings. What the structure of the new empire will be is not discussed. The question of 'theocracy' or mediation in the Book of Daniel is not yet ready to be pronounced on in this passage.

5. It may be doubted whether the Sibylline Oracles (which derive from the Hellenistic world) are conclusive in the closest sense for the apocalyptic context. But if III. 767 is drawn on at all, it should also be mentioned that the continuation in III 781f. says that the prophets of the Mighty God are then 'judges of mortal men and just kings'.

6. Since the Assumption of Moses is not fully extant, only cautious conclusions can be drawn about its eschatology. But if arguments are based on the appearance of the kingdom of God throughout his creation (10.1), ought not the succeeding verse,

> Then the hands of the angel shall be filled
> Who has been appointed chief,

to be considered too? The connection of the chief angel (Michael) with the kingdom could actually be the key to the understanding of the statement about the Son of man in Dan. 7 (cf. J. Coppens and L. Dequeker, *Le fils de l'homme et les Saints du Très-Haut en Daniel VII, dans les Apocryphes et dans le Nouveau Testament* [Analecta Lovaniensia Biblica et Orientalia III 23], 1961). Vielhauer's attempt at a proof grounded on the history of religion is therefore full of flaws in all the passages cited. We must ask, moreover, whether the idea of theocracy is not a typical notion of Hellenistic Israel. But this is not the place to pursue that question.

34. 'Gnosis is of the very spirit of apocalyptic.' R. Otto, *Reich Gottes und Menschensohn*, 1934, p.5 (ET, *The Kingdom of God and the Son of Man*, 1938, p.15), quoting Gressmann.

35. A passage out of the Syriac Apocalypse of Daniel, col. III/IV, is significant: 'The son shall speak to the father and say, "Thou art not my father". And the servant shall make himself equal to his lord. The maid shall be seated and the mistress shall serve. The youth shall lie down at table before him that is old'. The unpublished manuscript is being prepared for publication by my pupil H. Schmoldt.

36. Von Rad, *Theologie* II, p.224; II[4], p. 220; ET, p.212.

37. B. Violet, *Die Apokalypsen des Esra und des Baruch in deutscher Gestalt*, 1924, p.312 (on Vision VI, 19.14 [=II Bar. 74.1]).

38. The equivalents of the Hebrew root *glh* which are the basis of *apocalypsis/apokalyptein* mean the disclosure of a historical background which becomes known for the first time through the apocalypse in question. This is generally interpreted psychologically by present-day scholars, as the experience of 'divine' inspiration through the personality of the seer. But does that conform to the self-understanding of these men?

What they write is hardly revelation literature after the style of medieval mysticism (cf. J. Lindblom, *Die literarische Gattung der prophetischen Literatur*, 1924); it is rather a proclamation to a community, the writer merely acting as the messenger of a divine principal. What is laid bare is the eschatological drama, and that in such a fashion that the hearer or reader is in a position to make 'faith' the direction of his life, thereby making possible personal salvation at the impending divine coming. It is in so far that the theme is 'the revelation of the divine revelation'. Modern theology's concept of revelation, for which the Old Testament offers no analogy (cf. R. Rendtorff in *Offenbarung als Geschichte*, ed W. Pannenberg, 1965[3], pp. 21-41; ET, 'The Concept of Revelation in Ancient Israel', in *Revelation as History*, 1969, pp. 23-53) can in a sense be shown to be already present in apocalyptic.

39. See my article 'Spätisraelitisches Geschichtsdenken am Beispiel des Buches Daniel', *HZ* 193, 1961, p.7.

40. J.M. Schmidt, *Die jüdische Apokalyptik. Die Geschichte ihrer Erforschung von den Anfängen bis zu den Textfunden von Qumran*, 1969.

41. *RGG* I,[3]col. 463.

42. Hennecke–Schneemelcher II, p.411 (ET, p.586) therefore contemplates a further form, i.e., the farewell discourse - this, however, belonging to the same movement as the apocalypses themselves.

43. Nissen marshals five reasons for assigning Jubilees to the apocalypses (*op. cit.* p.246 n.6), none of which is entirely conclusive:

1. The secret revelation to a man of God - this already applies to Deuteronomy.

2. History is divided into periods - which is already the case among the Deuteronomists.

3. The Enoch tradition is taken over - but this is also true of the non-apocalyptic Ecclesiasticus.

4. Heavenly tablets appear to the seer. The motif crops up in I Enoch, where past and present history is inscribed on the tablets (81.2; 93.2; 106.19; 107.1). According to Jubilees, on the other hand, what is written on the tablets is primarily ritual and criminal law.

5. In 1.6-18, 22-26; 23.1-31, proper apocalypses allegedly appear. But is every Ezekiel-like combination of historical survey and prophecy actually an apocalypse?

Russell (*Method and Message*, p.54) is more cautious: 'Jubilees is not, strictly speaking, an apocalyptic book; but it belongs to the same milieu.'

44. Sources are cited in Burchard, *op. cit.* II, p.335f.

45. A.S.v.d. Woude, *Oudtestamentische Studiën* XIV, 1965, pp. 354-373; J.A. Fitzmyer, *JBL* 86, 1967, pp. 25-41.

46. A balanced consideration of the relationship between the Qumran community and apocalyptic can be found in Russell. Like Hanson, he holds Qumran to be 'a cooled-down apocalyptic sect' (*Method and Message*, p.24; see also his list of apocalyptic Qumran writings on p.39).

47. 'The apocalyptic literature of the Gaonic period is neither in form nor in matter a direct development of the pre-Talmudic Apocalypse', L.

Ginsberg, *JBL* 41, 1922, p.116 n.

48. The sole exception is to be found in Sanh. 9b, with a report of the discovery of a book in square script and in Hebrew - that is to say, a book with a canonical claim (Ginsberg, pp. 119f.)

49. E. Meyer, 'Ein neues Bruchstück Manethos über das Lamm des Bokchoris', *Zeitschrift für Ägyptische Sprache und Altertumkunde* 45, 1908/09, p.135f.

50. *Altorientalische Texte*, ed. by H. Gressmann, 1926,[2] pp.48f.; K. Koch, 'Das Lamm, das Ägypten vernichtet', *ZNW* 57, 1966,pp. 79-93.

51. Extensive material on this theme-complex, combined with exemplary reserve in the evaluation of it, can now be found in M. Hengel, *Judentum und Hellenismus* (WUNT 10, 1969), pp. 319-394, esp. pp. 335ff.

52. *Heil als Geschichte*, p.65 (ET, p.83).

CHAPTER IV

1. A. Hilgenfeld, *Die jüdische Apokalyptik in ihrer geschichtlichen Entwicklung*, 1857 (reprinted 1966), p.2. For the background of Hilgenfeld's views and their subsequent history cf. J.M. Schmidt, *Die jüdische Apokalyptik*, 1969, pp. 127ff.

2. B. Duhm, *Israels Propheten*, 1922,[2] p.460.

3. J. Wellhausen, *Israelitische und Jüdische Geschichte*, 1958,[9] p.175.

4. In his chapter on 'The Development of Judaism' Wellhausen also deals with apocalyptic and even commits himself to the statement: 'The book of Daniel has the same importance for historical scholarship as has the first chapter of Genesis for science' (p.286). This does not prevent him from viewing the book of Daniel as a revival of old folk beliefs 'which the Israelites had in common with the heathen' and which had 'retreated in the face of the monotheism of the prophets' (pp. 288f.).

5. E. Schürer, *Geschichte des jüdischen Volkes im Zeitalter Jesu Christi*, 3 vols., 1901ff.[3-4], reprinted 1964; ET, *A History of the Jewish People in the Time of Jesus Christ*, 5 vols., 1885-91.

6. J.M. Schmidt, *op. cit.*, p.174.

7. See above p.13.

8. 'Aus Wellhausens neuesten apokalyptischen Forschungen. Einige prinzipielle Erörterungen', *Zeitschrift für wissenschaftliche Theologie*, NF 7, 1889, pp. 581-611.

9. W. Klatt, *Hermann Gunkel* (FRLANT 100), 1969, pp. 36-40.

10. W. Klatt, 'Ein Brief von Hermann Gunkel . . .', *ZTK* 66, 1969, p.4.

11. *Theologie des Alten Testaments* I-III, 1933-39. Apocalyptic receives a brief mention in vol. I, pp. 208f. ('unfruitful other-worldly romanticism') and pp. 254f. (ET of 5th/6th ed. of 1959-64, *Theology of the Old Testament* I-II, 1961-67.)

12. *Theologie des Alten Testaments*, 1936, 1966[4] (ET of 1953[3], *Old Testament Theology*, 1957).

13. The commentary on Daniel in the Handbuch zum Alten Testament (1937) was written by a Dane, Aage Bentzen, and the one in Das Alte Testament Deutsch (1962) by a Scotsman, Norman Porteous (English ·

version in the Old Testament Library, 1965). The Swedish scholar Helmer Ringgren wrote 'Apokalyptik II. jüdische Apokalyptik' in *RGG* I[3] (cols. 464-6), and the same heading in the *Biblisch-historisches Handwörterbuch* was covered by the Norwegian A. Aalen.

14. *The Relevance of Apocalyptic,* 1944, rev. ed., 1946;*Apokalyptik, ihre Form und Bedeutung zur biblischen Zeit,* 1965.

15. *Das Geschichtsverständnis der alttestamentlichen Apokalyptik* (Arbeitsgemeinschaft für Forschung des Landes Nordrhein-Westfalen, Geisteswissenschaftliches Heft 21), 1954; reprinted in Noth, *Gesammelte Studien zum Alten Testament* (ThB 6), 1957, 1960[2], pp. 248-73; ET in *The Laws in the Pentateuch and Other Studies,* 1966, pp. 194-214.

16. *Op. cit.,* p.19, *Ges. St.* p. 265, ET, p.208; cf. p.24 (=pp. 270f.; ET, pp. 212f.).

17. *Ibid.,* p.25=p. 272; ET, p.214.

18. See my essay mentioned above, p.137 n. 39.

19. *Theokratie und Eschatologie* (WMANT 2), 1959.

20. *Op. cit.,* p.54.

21. *Ibid.,* p.59,

22. *Ibid.,* p.44.

23. *Ibid.,* p.136. Plöger applied his viewpoint to the exegesis of an apocalyptic book in his commentary on Daniel (Kommentar zum Alten Testament XVIII, 1965). Similar ideas may be found in O.H. Steck, 'Das Problem theologischer Strömungen in nachexilischer Zeit', *EvTH* 28, 1968, pp. 445-58.

24. *Gesetz und Geschichte, Untersuchungen zur Theologie der jüdischen Apokalyptik und der pharisäischen Orthodoxie* (WMANT 3), 1960.

25. *Op. cit.,* p. 109.

26. For a particularly detailed criticism see A. Nissen, 'Tora und Geschichte im Spätjudentum. Zu Thesen Dietrich Rösslers', *NovT* IX, 1967, pp. 241-77, see below p.87ff.

27. Rössler, *op. cit.,* p.68.

28. E.g., G. von Rad, 'Antwort auf Conzelmanns Fragen', *EvTH* 24, 1964, pp. 388-94, in reply to H. Conzelmann, 'Fragen an Gerhard von Rad', *ibid,* pp. 113-25. On Conzelmann's interpretation of apocalyptic, see below ch. VI.

29. *Theologie des Alten Testaments* II, 1960, pp. 314f.; ET of this edition, II, 1965, pp. 301f.

30. *Theologie* II, 1965[4], p. 319 (cf. ET, p. 303).

31. II, p. 319; ET, p. 306. This is softened in II[4], p. 317, to 'Something like an apotheosis of the teacher of Wisdom can be found'.

32. II[4], p. 329. Expectation of a resurrection is briefly apostrophized as apocalyptic in the paragraphs on the Psalms (*Theologie* I, 1957, p. 405; I[4], p. 420; ET I, 1962, p. 407).

33. II, p. 325, II[4], p. 334; ET, p. 312.

34. II, p. 326, II[4], p. 335; ET, p. 313.

35. II, p. 317; ET, p. 304; expanded in more detail in II[4], pp. 321f.

36. II, pp. 317f.; ET, pp. 304f.; II[4], p. 318.

37. II, p. 318, ET, p. 305. The subject of pseudonymity, which has frequently been considered by English scholars (see above, p.134 n.21) is dispatched by von Rad along the lines suggested by the views of nineteenth-century literary-critical school.

38. II⁴, pp. 320f.; cf. II, p. 319 (ET, p. 306).

39. Bultmann in *Geschichte und Eschatologie* (revised and expanded version of *History and Eschatology*, his Gifford Lectures of 1955), 1964, also talks about 'the dehistoricizing of history by apocalyptic' (p.35); but he gives a characteristically different reason from von Rad: 'Its end is determined by God and is not the organic close, the consummation of a course of development' (p.34). For Bultmann, therefore, it is the very contingent character of the end which makes him feel the lack of a historical mode of thought, whereas for von Rad the lack of contingency is decisive. (Incidentally the eschaton is hardly conceived in such absolute terms as Bultmann - on the basis of a misunderstood doctrine of the aeons - imagines; cf. my essay 'Der Schatz im Himmel', p.135 n.32 above.)

40. Cf. also the account of the Exodus in the apocalyptically influenced book of *Jannes and Jambres* (K. Koch, 'Das Lamm das Ägypten vernichtet', *ZNW* 57, 1966, pp. 79-93); or in Pseudo-Philo, which was probably also apocalyptically moulded.

41. *Theologie* II, p. 316; ET, p. 303; II⁴, p. 319, softens the phrase to 'This is impossible'.

42. II⁴, p. 327.

43. The term *sopher* has so many different colourings in the post-exilic period that it is rash simply to equate it with 'sage'. There is no doubt that Ecclus. 38. 34ff. presupposes the interpretation of Scripture as the *sopher's* task. But this was certainly not the function of a sage in previous centuries. Daniel is certainly classified among the *hakkamin* in the legends (which are apocalyptic in von Rad's view), but *hakam - hakkim* never appears as a title belonging to the apocalyptists particularly. It is quite possible that the apocalyptists allotted themselves a place in the ranks of the prophets (IV Ezra 7.129; Ass. Mos.1.5; Rev. 1.3; 22.9f.; 22.18f.). But, above all, the titles 'writer' and 'prophet' are interchangeable according to the evidence of the Targums; cf. O.H. Steck, *Israel und das gewaltsame Geschick der Propheten* (WMANT 23), 1967, p.96 n.4, cf. p.208.

44. This was brought out above all by von Rad's predecessor in Heidelberg, G. Hölscher, in 'Die Entstehung des Buches Daniel', *Theologische Studien und Kritiken*, 1919, pp. 113-39. On R.H. Pfeiffer cf. J.M. Schmidt, *op.cit.* (see n.1 above), p.260.

45. The only Wisdom writing where a reference to future salvation can be found is I Baruch (2.34f.; 4.30; 5.2-4), which von Rad does not quote. But how restrained and 'old fashioned' this eschatology is, compared with its apocalyptic counterpart, although I Baruch is much later than Daniel and Enoch!

46. *Theologie* II, p. 320; ET, p. 307.

47. II⁴, p. 328.

48. Of all the apocalypses, only I Enoch is 'encyclopaedic'; and it is on this book that von Rad principally bases his theory in the fourth edition.

But it is a question whether everything which is gathered together in I Enoch is in origin of an apocalyptic nature. We cannot exclude the possibility that whole Wisdom complexes were taken over and included *en block;* cf. von Rad himself, II,[4] p.323.

49. I, p. 99; I,[4] p. 105; ET, I, p.91.

50. I, pp. 349, 351; I[4], pp. 364f.; ET, I, pp.352, 354.

51. In order to avoid misunderstanding let me emphasize that my criticism of the chapter on apocalyptic by no means implies denial of the pioneer achievement of von Rad's total conception. See here my article 'Neuorientierung der alttestamentlichen Theologie', *Pastoralblätter* 101, 1961, pp. 548 - 59. (For considered objections to the unilateral derivation from Wisdom, see P. von der Osten-Sacken, *Die Apokalyptik in ihrem Verhältnis zu Prophetie und Weisheit* [Theologische Existenz heute 157], 1969. It is only a pity that the writer - without exegetical evidence - pronounces an undefined 'determinism' to be the centre of apocalyptic.)

52. O. Eissfeldt, *Einleitung in das Alte Testament*, 1934, p. 164; 1964[3], p. 109; ET, *The Old Testament: an Introduction*, 1965, p. 150.

53. *Ibid.*, 1934, p. 676; 1964[3], p. 841; ET, p. 620.

54. E. Sellin, *Einleitung in das Alte Testament*, 1965[10], completely revised and rewritten by G. Fohrer, p. 527; ET, *Introduction to the Old Testament*, New York 1968, London 1970, p. 479.

55. *Geschichte der israelitischen Religion*, 1969, p. 381.

CHAPTER V

1. Von Rad does cite Rowley in connection with the subject of pseudonymity (*Theologie* II, p. 318 n. 8; II,[4] p. 320 n. 13; ET, p. 305 n. 8), but without noting that Rowley definitely contests his own position (the camouflage hypothesis). A similar continental (i.e. German) narrowness of outlook in the treatment of important themes is incidentally censured by Wingren in connection with systematic theology in *TLZ* 93, 1968, cols. 81ff.

2. *Apoc. and Pseud.* II, p. vii.

3. *Ibid.*, II p. xi.

4. *Judaism* I - III, 1927-30; quotation from III, p. 18.

5. *Ibid.*

6. *The Pharisees*, 1924, p. 197.

7. *Ibid.*, p. 191.

8. *Ibid.*, p. 189.

9. A survey of the diligent research of British and American scholarship is given by J.C. Rylaarsdam, 'Intertestamental Studies since Charles' *Apocrypha and Pseudepigrapha*', in *The Study of the Bible Today and Tomorrow*, ed. H.R. Willoughby, 1947, pp. 32-51. The literature on apocalyptic, however, gets only cursory treatment.

10. *The Relevance of Apocalyptic*, 1944, p.35.

11. *Ibid.*, p. 41.

12. *Ibid.*, p. 155.

13. *Ibid.*, p. 168.

14. *Ibid.*, p. 162.

15. *Ibid.*, pp. 172-4.

16. The agreement of prophetic and apocalyptic eschatology is stressed by, for example, G.E. Ladd, 'Why not Prophetic-Apocalyptic?', *JBL* 76, 1957, pp. 192-200, and by B. Vawter, 'Apocalyptic: its Relation to Prophecy', *CBQ* 22, 1960, pp. 33-46.

17. *Old Testament Apocalyptic*, 1952, p. 8.

18. 'Apocalyptic and History', in *The Bible and Modern Scholarship*, ed. J.P. Hyatt, 1965, pp. 98-113; quotation from p. 112.

19. Frost merely quotes at the beginning passages from IV Ezra, and only from the introductory visions, where the seer puts the problems in speech and counter-speech - in contrast to the solutions of the final visions.

20. *The Method and Message of Jewish Apocalyptic*, 1964, pp. 21f.

21. Quoted by T.W. Manson, 'Some Reflections on Apocalyptic', in *Aux sources de la tradition chrétienne: mélanges offerts à M. Goguel*, 1950, p. 142 (the whole passage quoted by D.S. Russell, *op. cit.*, p. 84). Like nearly all English scholars, Manson presupposes that there was a deep distinction between apocalyptic and rabbinism, both of which make use of prophecy in their own way and both of which throw the origin of their systems of interpretation back to 'the remote past' (the rabbis to the oral Torah stemming from Sinai). Manson tries to see the two as mutually complementary systematic systems, which through their union created Judaism.

22. Russell, *op. cit.*, pp. 95, 97, taking the quotation from Manson, *op. cit.*, p. 142.

23. *Op. cit.*, p. 9. Russell has expressed his ideas in shorter form in the second part of his book *Between the Testaments*, 1959.

24. F.C. Burkitt, *Judaism and the Beginnings of Christianity* II, 1923, pp. 51ff.

25. William Manson, *Jesus the Messiah*, 1943, p. 12.

26. *Ibid.*, p. 13.

27. *Ibid.*, p. 16.

28. 'Apocalyptic and Pharisaism', *ExpT* 59, 1958, pp. 233-7, reprinted in *Christian Origins and Judaism*, 1962, pp. 19-30; quotation from *Origins*, p. 20.

29. In order to protect the picture of Jesus from a mythological interpretation, Davies goes a step further and smoothes out the gulf between apocalyptic and Pharisaism, so much discussed by English Old Testament scholars, by means of the following arguments: (*a*) the Torah enjoyed the same esteem among both parties; (*b*) the eschatological teaching was common to both − the travail of the messianic times, the gathering of the exiles, the days of the Messiah, the new Jerusalem, the Judgment, Gehenna, the resurrection. Where was the expectation of the advent of the Messiah stronger than in Rabbi Aqiba, the champion of Bar Kochba? 'Nothing could more point to the reality of eschatological belief among the Rabbis and to the falsity of the customary distinction between

fanatic Apocalypticism and sober orthodoxy' (*Origins*, pp. 22f).

It is revealing of the path followed by English-speaking scholars that Davies' authority, the American Louis Ginsberg, judged quite differently: the rabbis 'did not fail to see in the wild and vague visions of those dreamers a true menace to the physical and spiritual welfare of Israel' ('Some Observations on the Attitude of the Synagogue towards the Apocalyptic - Eschatological Writings', *JBL* 41, 1922, p.134).

30. *Heil als Geschichte*, 1965, p.207; ET, *Salvation in History*, 1967, p. 229.

31. *The New Testament Background: Selected Texts*, 1956, p. 227.

32. *Jesus and the Gospel Tradition*, 1967, pp. 94, 99.

33. *Ibid.*, pp. 42-5.

34. *Ibid.*, p. 41.

35. G. Haufe, *TLZ* 93, 1968, col. 750.

CHAPTER VI

1. *Die Predigt Jesus vom Reiche Gottes*, 1892, pp. 61-3; ET, 1971, pp. 133ff.

2. *Das Messianitäts - und Leidensgeheimnis*, 1901 (reprinted 1956), p. 28; ET, *The Mystery of the Kingdom of God: the Secret of Jesus' Messiahship and Passion*, 1925 (reprinted 1950), p. 67.

3. *Die Mystik des Apostels Paulus*, 1930; ET, 1931.

4. *Die jüdische Apokalyptik, ihre religionsgeschichtliche Herkunft und ihre Bedeutung für das Neue Testament*, 1903, p.56.

5. 'The clearer our grasp of the nature of the contemporary Jewish hope, the more obvious it becomes how individual the path was which Jesus struck out in his preaching about the kingdom of God . . . With the sure touch of a master he spiritualized the popular belief in the kingdom of God by de-nationalizing it almost entirely. In this way he deepened it immensely, religiously and ethically, and at the same time individualized it' (*ibid.*, p.52). On Bousset's reaction (as well as Gunkel's) cf. W.G. Kümmel, *Das Neue Testament. Geschichte der Erforschung seiner Probleme*, 1958, pp. 291-4.

6. For a characteristic example see W. Mundle, 'Das religiöse Problem des IV. Esrabuches', *ZAW* 47, 1929, pp. 222-49. His thesis is that 'It is the ideas of Pharisaic Judaism which meet us everywhere in these apocalypses' (p.223). Mundle arrives at this surprising conclusion by reading the idea of the law into all possible statements, but by flatly postulating, wherever the mood seems to be 'far from the naïve certainty of salvation characteristic of unbroken Jewish piety', that 'one must not give too much weight to these statements' (p.241). The writer's pen is all too obviously guided by the apologetic motive of setting IV Ezra at as far a remove as possible from Paul.

7. J. Jeremias, *Jerusalem zur Zeit Jesu* II.1, 1929, p.107; 1962[3], pp.271f; ET, *Jerusalem in the Time of Jesus*, 1969, pp. 238f.

8. In their *Kommentar zum Neuen Testament aus Talmud und Midrasch*, 5 vols., 1922-56.

144 The Rediscovery of Apocalyptic

9. *Op. cit.*, 1926, p.14.

10. *Ibid.*, p. 125.

11. *TWNT* I, 1933, pp. 570-3; *TDNT* I, pp. 571-4.

12. *TWNT* II, 1935, pp. 130f.; *TDNT* II, pp. 127f.

13. *TWNT* II, p. 199; *TDNT* II, p. 197.

14. *TWNT* III, 1938, p. 580; *TDNT* III, p. 578.

15. *TWNT* VII, 1964, pp. 497ff.

16. *TWNT* VIII, 1969, pp. 403ff.

17. *Christus und die Zeit*, 1946, pp. 70-81, esp. p. 71; ET, *Christ and Time*, rev. ed., 1962, pp. 81-93, esp. pp. 82f.

18. 'Die Offenbarung des Johannes 1920-1934', *TR*, NF 6, 1934, pp. 269-314, and *ibid.*, 7, 1935, pp. 28-62; quotation from *TR* 6, p. 270.

19. *Ibid.*, pp. 286ff.

20. *TR* 7, p. 62.

21. *TR* 6, p. 306.

22. *Das Urchristentum im Rahmen der antiken Religionen*, 1949, p.91; ET, *Primitive Christianity in its Contemporary Setting*, 1956, p. 82.

23. *Theologie des Neuen Testamentes*, 1953, p. 4; ET, *Theology of the New Testament* I, 1952, pp. 5f.

24. So *ibid.*, pp. 108f. (ET, pp. 109f.), and section 15. For a time Bultmann saw Gnosticism as the encroaching movement. He reckoned with the likelihood that 'Jewish apocalyptic was already influenced' by Gnosticism, which - via apocalyptic - would thus have influenced Paul as well (*RGG* IV,[2]col. 1030).

25. *Reich Gottes und Menschensohn*, 1934, pp. 3f.; ET, *The Kingdom of God and the Son of Man*, 1938, p. 14. Otto himself tells us that when he wrote his early book *Leben und Wirken Jesu*, 1901, he 'much underestimated the great spiritual content of late Jewish apocalyptic'. If this is different in his later book, the change is connected with his dogmatic interest in bringing out the Holy One as the 'wholly other'; here apocalyptic dualism fits in excellently. Cf. *Reich Gottes*, p. 35 note and p. 30 (ET, p. 48 note and pp. 40f.).

26. *Theologie des Neuen Testamentes*, 1941, p. 6; ET, *New Testament Theology*, 1955, p. 21. After the Second World War, Stauffer altered the direction of his views, perhaps in an aggressive defence against the ideas of the Bultmann school: 'Jesus' message is primarily a message about today, a *kairos* message. In this it differs fundamentally from the apocalyptic messages of his day, and even from the message of John the Baptist. "The kingdom of God is in the midst of you." ' Jesus' supporters did not understand this because they were too deeply infected by vulgar apocalyptic ideas. That is the reason for the unfortunate thing that happened after the death of Jesus: 'Now the eschatological fever breaks out without restraint, infecting ever wider circles (Acts 2. 39ff.). The first apostles, Paul, James, Justus, the brothers of the Lord - all were seized by it' (*Jesus*, Dalphtaschenbücher 332, 1957, pp. 118ff.).

27. Feine-Behm-Kümmel, *Einleitung in das Neue Testament*, 1965[14], p. 348; ET, W.G. Kümmel, *Introduction to the New Testament*, 1966, p. 333.

28. *Fragen zur Geschichtlichkeit Jesu*, 1966, p.107.

29. *Gottes Herrschaft und Reich*, 1959, p. 43; ET, *God's Rule and Kingdom*. 1963, p.69.

30. *Ibid.*, p. 47; ET, pp. 74f.

31. *Ibid.*, p. 56; ET, p.87.

32. *Ibid.*, p. 62; ET, p. 95.

33. *Ibid.*, p. 64; ET. p. 97

34. *Lexikon für Theologie und Kirche* I, 1957, p. 697.

35. *Offenbarung und Heilsgeschehen* (BevTh 7), 1941, pp. 27-69, reprinted in *Kerygma und Mythos*, ed. H.W. Bartsch (Theologische Forschung 1), 1948, pp. 15-48; ET in *Kerygma and Myth*, 1953, pp. 1-44.

36. *Kerygma und Mythos*, p. 26; ET, pp. 15f.

37. *Ibid.*, p. 18; ET, p. 5.

38. *Ibid.*, p. 23; ET, pp. 11f.

39. *Ibid.*, p. 29; ET, p. 20.

40. Cf. J.M. Robinson, *A New Quest of the Historical Jesus*, 1959.

41. 'Gottesreich und Menschensohn in der Verkündigung Jesu', *Festschrift für G. Dehn*, 1957, pp. 51-79, reprinted in *Aufsätze zum Neuen Testament* (ThB 31), 1965, pp. 55-91; 'Jesus und der Menschensohn', *ZTK* 60, 1963, pp. 133-77, reprinted in *Aufsätze*, pp. 92-140.

42. *Dehn Festschrift*, p. 78, *ZTK*, p. 139. Two reasons are given. (1) In the synoptic gospels it is noticeable that 'Where the Son of man is an individual figure and plays an active role, nothing is said about the kingdom of God. The Son of man is not an integral part of the hope for the eschatological rule of God' (*Festschrift*, p. 76). It is true that the two powers are hardly combined in Q. But to interpret by means of a 'principle of contradiction' hardly does justice to the complex questions arising from the history of the tradition; cf. H.E. Tödt, *Der Menschensohn in der synoptischen Überlieferung*, 1959, pp. 313f.; ET, *The Son of Man in the Synoptic Tradition*, 1965, pp. 344f. (2) The only texts at our disposal for the pre-Christian period are the apocalypses. In these too 'a purely "theocratic" conception runs parallel to one involving End - time functionaries; there is nowhere a mixture of the two conceptions'; it is only manufactured retrospectively in IV Ezra 7 (*ZTK*, p. 176). This assertion is untenable, however; cf. pp.135f. n. 33 above

43. We only have to consider a hypothetical case: what would remain of Luther if one denied him every theme which can also be attested as medieval or early Protestant? If in Jesus' case more has been left up to now, that could be due to the fragmentary state of the comparable texts at our disposal. It is rather difficult to see why supporters of the reduction method hold fast so obstinately to the idea of the sovereignty of God as being Jesus' own; as if the relevant synoptic statements with their modification of this idea were further removed from the apocalypses than their corresponding statements about the Son of man. Perhaps a reliable criterion for distinguishing the genuine sayings of Jesus can be found by linguistic and formal observations - i.e., through form criticism; but the reduction method, as it is usually applied, has nothing in common with form criticism.

44. Bultmann, *Theologie des Neuen Testaments*, p. 6; ET *Theology of the New Testament* I, p. 7.

45. K.L. Schmidt in *TWNT* I, p. 583, lines 32f.; *TDNT* I, p. 583.

46. M. Werner, *Die Entstehung des christlichen Dogmas*, 1953[2], p. 47; cf. abridged English ed., *The Formation of Christian Dogma*, 1957, p.14.

47. *Ibid.*, p. 50 (English omits).

48. *Lehrbuch der Dogmengeschichte* I-III, 1931[5]; ET of 3rd edition, *History of Dogma* I-VII, 1894-99; quotation from I, p. 114 (ET I, p. 101).

49. *Op. cit.*, p. 8.

50. E. Grässer, *Das Problem der Parusieverzögerung in den synoptischen Evangelien und der Apostelgeschichte* (BZNW 22), 1957, p. 16: 'The problem presented by the delay of the parousia had its fixed place in the redaction of the evangelists.' Cf. H. Conzelmann, 'Parousie', in *RGG* V[3], cols. 130-32 (bibliog.).

51. W.G. Kümmel, *Verheissung und Erfüllung*, 1954, 1956[3], ET, *Promise and Fulfilment*, 1957, was the first important answer to Werner. Kümmel does not allow the apocalyptic background to present a problem *per se*. The schematic picture of apocalyptic as a useless speculation about the future is so consistently presupposed that, for example, the intention of teaching people what they ought to do in face of the impending end becomes in the eschatological discourse in Matt. 25. 31ff. the 'proof' (p. 88; ET, p. 95) of a fundamental detachment from apocalyptic. This method even permits Kümmel to arrive at the conclusion that Jesus' eschatological message 'stands in complete contrast to the "Weltanschauung" of apocalyptic' (p. 97; ET, p. 104)!

52. 'Die Bekehrung des Paulus als religionsgeschichtliche Problem', *ZTK* 56, 1959, pp. 273-93; quotation from p. 277.

53. Cf. pp. 41f. above.

54. *ZTK* 56, p. 285.

55. 'Das Offenbarungsverständnis in der Geschichte des Urchristentums', in *Offenbarung als Geschichte*, ed. W. Pannenberg (Beiheft zu Kerygma und Dogma 1), 1961, 1963[3], pp. 42-90; ET, 'The Understanding of Revelation within Primitive Christianity', *Revelation as History*, 1969, pp. 55-121; quotation from p. 48 (ET, p. 63).

56. *Ibid.*, p. 53; ET, p. 70.

57. *Ibid.*, p. 54 n. 31; ET omits.

58. *Ibid.*, p. 61; ET, p. 79.

59. *Ibid.*, p. 90; ET, p. 114. Wilckens has meanwhile modified his views and emphasizes the difference between the early Palestinian and Hellenistic churches; cf. 'Jesusüberlieferung und Christuskerygma: zwei Wege urchristlicher Überlieferungsgeschichte', *Theologia Viatorum* 10, 1966, pp. 310-99.

60. See ch. VII.2, pp. 101ff. below.

61. 'Die Anfänge christlicher Theologie', *ZTK*, 57, 1960, pp. 160-185, reprinted in *Exegetische Versuche und Besinnungen* II, 1964[2], pp. 82-104; ET in *New Testament Questions of Today*, 1969, pp. 82-107, quotation from *ZTK*, p.180; ET, p.102.

62. *ZTK* p. 175; ET, p. 96.

63. *ZTK*, pp. 175f.; ET, p. 97.

64. *ZTK*, pp. 182f.; ET, p. 105.

65. *ZTK*, p. 176; ET, p. 98.
66. *ZTK*, p. 179; ET, p. 101.
67. *ZTK*, pp. 184f.; ET, p. 107.
68. *Auslegung der Apokalypse Johannes* (a lecture delivered in Mainz in the winter semester 1948-49).
69. The theories of Rössler, Wilckens and Käsemann are, however, cautiously acknowledged by O. Cullmann as being 'a fitting reaction' (*Heil als Geschichte*, 1965, p.63; ET, *Salvation in History*, 1967, p.81). G. Klein, on the other hand, emphatically rejects their views, cf. *Monatsschrift für Pastoraltheologie* 51, 1962, pp. 65-88 and his *Theologie des Wortes Gottes und die Hypothese der Universalgeschichte* (BevTH 37), 1964.
70. *ZTK* 58, 1961, pp. 227-244, reprinted in *Wort und Glaube* II, 1969, pp. 72-91, quotation from *ZTK*, p. 230.
71. *Ibid.*, pp. 231f.
72. *Ibid.*, p. 236.
73. *Ibid.*, p. 240.
74. *Ibid.*, pp. 240f.
75. *Ibid.*, p. 242.
76. 'Über die Aufgabe einer christlichen Theologie', *ZTK* 58, 1961, pp. 245-67.
77. *Ibid.*, p. 251.
78. *Ibid.*, p. 255.
79. *Ibid.*, pp. 254f.
80. *Ibid.*, p. 256.
81. *Ibid.*, p. 267.
82. 'Zum Thema der urchristlichen Apokalyptik', *ZTK* 59, 1962, pp. 257-84, reprinted in *Exegetische Versuche und Besinnungen* II, 1964[2], pp. 105-31; ET in *New Testament Questions of Today*, 1969, pp. 108-37.
83. *ZTK*, p. 263; ET, p. 114.
84. *ZTK*, p. 278; ET, p. 131.
85. *ZTK*, p. 283; ET, p. 136.
86. *ZTK*, p. 268 n. 2; ET omits. Käsemann's tone is even sharper where Fuchs mocks concrete apocalyptic ideas, such as the notion of the Last Judgment (see above): 'I can very well imagine a fit of rage in Fuchs, but not in the universal Judge. The imagination of a historian has certain limits' (p. 265 n. 1).
87. 'Zur Analyse der Bekenntnisformel I Cor. 15.3-5', *EvTh* 25, 1965, pp. 1-11.
88. *Ibid.*, p.9.
89. *Ibid.*, p. 3 n. 16.
90. 'Konsequente Traditionsgeschichte?', *ZTK* 62, 1965, pp. 137-52; quotation from p. 139.
91. 'Ist Apokalyptik die Mutter der christlichen Theologie?', in *Apophoreta: Festschrift für E. Haenchen* (BZNW 30), 1964, pp. 64-69; reprinted in *Exegetica*, 1967, pp. 476-82.
92. *Apophoreta*, p. 69.
93. For Daniel the world's history of sin is a preparation for the era of

grace, rather as it is for Paul. See my article 'Spätisraelitisches Geschichtsverständnis', *HZ* 193, 1961, pp. 24f.

94. *Geschichte und Eschatologie*, 1964[2], p. 38, the revised and expanded German edition of his Gifford Lectures of 1955, *History and Eschatology*, 1957, pp. 32f. In the first quotation the German edition differs slightly from the English, mainly through the addition of the important word 'only'.

95. Hennecke-Schneemelcher (see ch. II n. 4 above) II, pp. 428-54; ET, pp. 608-42. Vielhauer admittedly supports a view of apocalyptic which was in force before the First World War. He therefore finds it an easy matter to remove Jesus from any conceivable apocalyptic framework.

96. 'Apokalyptik und Typologie bei Paulus', *TLZ* 89, 1964, cols. 321-44; reprinted in *Christologie und Ethik*, 1968, pp. 234-67.

97. *TLZ*, p. 328.

98. *Ibid.*, p. 343.

99. *Gerechtigkeit Gottes bei Paulus* (FRLANT 87), 1965, p. 238.

100. *Ibid.*, p. 175.

101. *Ibid.*, p. 166.

102. *Kerygma und Apokalyptik*, 1967, p.7. See also his first book, *Die apokalyptische Sendung Jesu*, 1962.

103. *Kerygma und Apokalyptik*, p. 39.

104. *Ibid.*, p. 37.

105. I have considered the methodological questions raised by these articles of Nissen, Betz and Murdock in more detail in an essay 'Zur Exegese apokalyptischer Texte', which will appear shortly.

106. 'Tora und Geschichte im Spätjudentum: zu Thesen D. Rösslers', *NovT* IX, 1967, pp. 241-77.

107. Nissen does not shrink from crass misrepresentation in his account of the literature. For instance, Rössler, *Gesetz und Geschichte*, p.11, had written earlier in connection with the plan of his work: 'Thus the question of the *Sitz im Leben*, i.e., the historical background of the apocalyptic texts, must remain undiscussed. . .' It is certainly legitimate to ask whether here the grapes have not become too sour for the fox, and whether the delicate question of the *Sitz im Leben* has been left out, not only for reasons of space, but also because of the obscure state of scholarly opinion. But what must not be done by anyone who wants to be taken seriously as a scholar, is to deduce from this, like Nissen (p. 243 n. 4), 'the deliberate renunciation of historical method' (a reproach which would today disqualify absolutely every commentator). It is even less permissible when, like Nissen, one is oneself dispensing with all discussion of the *Sitz im Leben* of apocalyptic. It may be mentioned in passing that Nissen (according to p. 275 n. 2) has read my article of Daniel (see above, p. 137 n. 39) equally superficially, at least feeling it unnecessary to reconsider in the original text passages I have quoted.

108. Nissen, *op. cit.*, p. 244 n. 2.

109. *Ibid*, p. 249, based on a remark made by de Faye in 1892. Nissen finds such judgments so reliable that he feels entirely free to avoid an individual interpretation of the primary text.

110. *Ibid.*, p. 252, citing Jocz. Incidentally a stay in Israel and a conversation with an educated Israeli would speedily acquaint Nissen with a very different Jewish opinion.

111. *Ibid.*, pp. 254f.

112. *Ibid.*, p. 267 n. 2. How does this sentence fit in with the one on p. 246, according to which the apocalypses are not a genre but 'hybrid products'?

113. *Ibid.*, p. 277.

114. *Ibid.*, pp. 271f.

115. *Journal for Theology and the Church* 6, 1969, pp. 192-207; simultaneously as 'Das Verständnis der Apokalyptik in der Theologie der Pannenberg-Gruppe', *ZTK* 65, 1968, pp. 257-70. Betz feels that where apocalyptic becomes the hinge of the two Testaments, as it is for Pannenberg and his friends, an Old Testament theology is assigned the goal of following what is said about revelation and the knowledge of Yahweh from its pre-Israelite roots down to that point where the ultimate revelation is only expected in the future. It is a pity that Betz does not give way to this feeling but rejects it from the outset (pp. 193f.).

116. *Ibid.*, p. 206.

117. *Ibid.*, p. 202.

118. *Ibid.*, p. 206.

119. *Ibid.*, p. 205.

120. *Ibid.*, p. 203.

121. *Ibid.*, p. 201.

122. *Ibid.*, pp. 196f. He goes on: 'Rössler seems unaware of the fact that even in his own formulation we are dealing not with salvation history but with cosmology and astrology.' The antithesis presupposes that Betz can only conceive 'salvation history' in the sense of nineteenth-century positive or pietistic theology. A salvation history of which 'natural history' is a part is for him inconceivable. With this he of course makes it impossible for the commentator to apply the term 'salvation history' to any Old Testament facts at all, since there, from the Yahwist onwards at the latest, 'natural history' is the necessary preliminary for the history of mankind as well as the history of Israel.

123. *Ibid.*, p. 198.

124. F. König is sceptical about Iranian influences (*Zarathustras Jenseitsvorstellungen und das Alte Testament*, 1964). W. Bousset, on the other hand, was thoroughly convinced that 'the new factor which Jewish apocalyptic introduced into the Jewish hope was conditioned and inspired by the Iranian religion' (*Die jüdische Apokalyptik*, 1903, p. 45).

125. Cf. C. Colpe, *TWNT* VIII, pp. 403-81.

126. 'Zum Problem der religionsgeschichtlichen Verständnisses der Apokalyptik', *ZTK* 63, 1966, pp. 391-409. Note the questions which are still open (p. 408)! Equally meagre results are to be found in C.C. McCown, 'Hebrew and Egypt Apocalyptic Literature, *Harvard Theological Review* 18, 1925, pp. 357-411, and W.W. Hallo, 'Akkadian Apocalypses', *Israel Exploration Journal* 16, 1966, pp. 231-42.

127. *Interpretation* 21, 1967, pp. 167-87.

128. *Op. cit.*, p. 173.
129. *Ibid.*, pp. 170f.
130. See my article, 'Spätisraelitisches Geschichtsdenken am Beispiel des Buches Daniel', *HZ* 193, 1961, p. 7.
131. Murdock, *op. cit.*, p. 186.
132. See above p. 26, paragraph iv.
133. *Neutestamentliche Zeitgeschichte*, 1965, p. 126; ET, 1969, p. 170.
134. *Ibid.*, p. 217; ET, p. 290.
135. See n. 27 above.
136. On the form versus matter scheme see my observations in 'Der Tod des Religionsstifters', *KuD* 8, 1962, p. 101.
137. *Einleitung in das Neue Testament*, 1963, 1965[3], p. 229; ET, 1968, p. 273.
138. *Grundriss der neutestamentlichen Theologie*, 1967, p. 178; ET, 1969, pp. 157f.
139. *Ibid.*, p. 344 n. 11; ET, p. 313 n. 3.
140. *Revue de l'Histoire des Religions* 106, 1932, pp. 381-434, 489-524; quotation from p. 387.
141. *Ibid.*, p. 383.
142. *Le Judaisme avant Jésus-Christ*, 1931, pp. 70-81.
143. *Ibid.*, pp. 81-90.
144. *Ibid.*, p. 72.
145. *Ibid.*, p. xi.
146. *Ibid.*, pp. xxiif.
147. *Ibid.*, p. 267.
148. *Le Judaisme palestinien au temps de Jésus-Christ*, 1935; in the shortened version of 1950, p. 9.
149. *Ibid.*, p. 12.
150. *La Bible apocryphe: 1. En marge de l'Ancien Testament*, tr. J. Bonsirven, 1952; *2. Evangiles apocryphes*, tr. F. Amiot, 1953 [this work not available to me; Daniel-Rops quoted from the German version, *Die apokryphe Bibel am Rande des Alten Testaments*, 1959, pp. 17, 27]. The excommunicated outsider A. Loisy presents another view: in his commentary *L'Apocalypse de Jean*, 1923, he describes the book of Revelation as being the summing up of primitive Christian eschatology fed by earlier and later Jewish prophecy (cf. Lohmeyer, *TR*, NF 6, 1934, p. 296).
151. *Les Sectes Juives au temps de Jésus*, 1960, p. 9.
152. Cited by Eusebius, *Ecclesiastical History* IV, 22.7.
153. *Les dires prophétiques d'Esdras*, 1938, pp. viif.

CHAPTER VII.

1. *Das eschatologische Denken der Gegenwart*, 1936, p. 7.
2. H.E. Weber, quoted by Holmström, *op. cit.*, p. 17.
3. *Der Römerbrief*, 1922[2], p. 298; cf. ET of sixth edition, 1933, p. 314.
4. Holmström, *op. cit.*, p. 1.
5. *Die Bedeutung der Eschatologie für die neuere protestantische*

Theologie, 1935, p. 49.

6. *Ibid.*, p. 162.

7. *Ibid.*, p. 163.

8. 'Heilsgeschehen und Geschichte', *KuD* 5, 1959, pp. 218-37, 259-88; reprinted in *Grundfragen systematischer Theologie*, 1967, pp. 22-78; ET in *Basic Questions in Theology* I, 1970, pp. 15-80.

9. *KuD*, p. 222; ET, p. 20.

10. *Offenbarung als Geschichte* (Beiheft to *KuD* 1), 1963²; ET, *Revelation as History*, 1969, pp. 125-58; quotation from p. 91; ET, p. 125.

11. *Ibid.*, pp. 95f.; ET, pp. 131-3.

12. *Ibid.*, p. 92; ET, p. 127.

13. *Ibid.*, p. 141; ET, p. 193.

14. *Ibid.*, p. 142; ET, p. 193.

15. *Grundzüge der Christologie*, 1966², p. 62; ET, *Jesus - God and Man*, 1968, p. 67.

16. *Was ist der Mensch?*, 1962; see p. 33 on the resurrection.

17. See the discussion in *Theology as History* (New Frontiers in Theology 3). ed. J.M. Robinson and J.B. Cobb, 1967.

18. See above on von Rad (pp. 42f.), Frost (pp. 52f.) and Nissen (pp. 87ff.).

19. In his *Grundzüge der Christologie* (ET, *Jesus - God and Man*), Pannenberg explores with considerable exegetical penetration 'The Significance of Jesus' Resurrection' in the context of the history of traditions of primitive Christianity (pp. 61-69; ET, pp. 66-73). He had previously brought out, in contrast to the Bultmann school, that Jesus' claim to complete authority is not to be understood in timeless isolation but is directed towards a subsequent divine confirmation (p.61; ET, p. 66). But the more detailed explanation already seems dubious: 'This claim by Jesus could be shown to be true only when the general resurrection of the dead occurred and the judgment of the Son of Man actually took place' (p. 59; ET, p. 64). Is not the fulfilment of Jesus' prophecies (and hence the confirmation of his person and destiny) expected primarily through the coming of the Kingdom? Is it permissible to stress the resurrection in this way in the context of the historical Jesus as being one of two decisive elements for the eschaton? The conclusion which Pannenberg's interpretation draws as regards the history of the tradition does not seem very convincing either: 'Then when his disciples were confronted by the resurrected Jesus, they no doubt[!] also understood this as the beginning of the universal resurrection of the dead' (p.61; ET, p. 66). Did they? Does not the idea of exaltation play an important role - perhaps an even more important one? If this were so the resurrection of Jesus would not, it is true, have necessarily ceased to belong within the apocalyptic expectation for those involved; but it would certainly have lost a good part of its proleptic character.

20. G. Klein in *Theologie des Wortes Gottes und die Hypothese der Universalgeschichte* (BevTH 37), 1964, criticizes on pp. 24-37 Pannenberg's assimilation of apocalyptic in his interpretation of the

resurrection. Klein produces considerable grounds for maintaining that in the New Testament the resurrection of Jesus does not count as the substantiation of a claim (p. 25 n. 22). He also disputes the axiomatic character of the resurrection for apocalyptically minded contemporaries (p. 29 n. 25). But Klein is on dangerous ground when he maintains that a relation between the Christian message of the resurrection and the apocalyptic hope merely proves a relation 'between Christian and a branch of Jewish language'. The linguistic form is accounted completely unimportant. 'If this reality had a truly all-conquering character, how was it dependent, and how did it remain dependent, on a particular context of ideas, in order to achieve its revelatory effect?' (p.31). Can a historically-minded theologian today really tear language and reality apart in this naive way? Though the same naiveté allows Klein in another passage to talk as a matter of course about the 'sovereign *verbum alienum*' (p.23), and to use that as an adequate argument.

21. *Theologie der Hoffnung* (1964), 1968[7]; ET of 5th edition, 1965.

22. The point of contact between Pannenberg and Moltmann, the interest of both in apocalyptic, may perhaps be connected with the fact that the two worked side by side in the theological college in Wuppertal.

23. Moltmann, *op. cit.*, p. 16; ET, pp. 20f.

24. *Ibid.*, p. 13; ET, p. 18.

25. *Ibid.*, pp. 123f.; ET, pp. 136f.

26. *Ibid.*, p. 124; ET, pp. 137f.

27. *Zukunft und Verheissung*, 1965, p. 96.

28. *Ibid.*, p. 233.

29. *Ibid.*, p. 367.

30. *Ibid.*, p. 368.

31. *Ibid.*, p. 46.

32. *Ibid.*, p. 229.

33. *Dogmatik*, 1962=1967.[2] Trillhaas does treat the heading eschatology on 60 pages (pp. 441-501), thereby giving more space to the subject than to the Holy Spirit (pp. 405-440); and he even lists the characteristics of apocalyptic (pp. 446-450). But all 'cosmological' eschatology is excluded from the Christian hope as being irrelevant. What is behind this is the common and naive contemporary opinion that the present can be perceived with sufficient certainty without historical aspects being necessary. 'The present is for us the watershed between what we know with comparative certainty and the future Unknown. Even what has been . . . recedes backwards into darkness.' Consequently for us the eschatological question has changed: 'The present takes on an eminent significance. Inasmuch as we know ourselves to be between past and future, we know ourselves in our present. And it is in this present that our decision is made before God' (p. 469). Trillhaas therefore does not need any theology of history. 'The salvation-history framework, which bound together this history of ancient Israel, the history of the nations, and the history, as well as the future, of the church, into a surveyable unity becomes completely insubstantial according to this view of things. Individual eschatology takes its place. Eschatology ceases to be a

historical, or end-historical, myth and becomes an existential question' (p.471).

34. *Interpretation* 14, 1960, pp. 131-42.

35. *Op. cit.*, p. 131.

36. *Ibid.*, p. 132.

37. *Ibid.*, p. 142.

38. The German line is emphatically taken over by Harvey Cox, who understands God not as the One who is but as He that is to come, and sees the task of theology as lying in the political field, not the religious one. It is this which is for Cox the meaning of prophecy. In *On Not Leaving it to the Snake* (1968) he expounds his theory that Christianity contained three contradictory expectations of the future: 'The *apocalyptic*, deriving from ancient near Eastern dualism, foresees imminent catastrophe, produces a negative evaluation of this world, and often believes in an elite which will be snatched from the inferno . . . *Teleology*, derived mainly from the Greeks . . . sees the future as the unwinding of a purpose. . . . The *prophetic* is the characteristically Hebrew notion of the future as the open field of human hope and responsibility' (p.36). Since the three views are still rivals in both their Christian and their secularized forms, the apocalyptic attitude is described in more detail: 'Apocalypticism and politics are inherently incompatible . . . (For apocalypticism) rational action is useless because powers outside history and beyond human control will quickly bring the whole thing to a blazing end . . . Apocalypticism is at work wherever people simply decide to opt out of the political process and seek personal salvation or wait for the deluge' (pp. 38f.). It is evident that Cox has not only borrowed systematic ideas from the continent; he has also faithfully taken over the stereotypes of German biblical scholarship.

CHAPTER VIII

1. Published by J. Foret, Paris, 1961, and advertised as the 'most valuable' and the 'heaviest' book on the world (it weights 210 kg., i.e., over 4 cwt.).

2. The German text may also be found in E. Jünger, *Werke* (n.d.), pp. 334f.

3. E.g., Heidegger, *Holzwege*, 1950,[2] pp.202f.

4. *Der philosophische Glaube*, 1948, p. 38; ET, *The Perennial Scope of Philosophy*, 1950, p. 42.

5. *Vom Ursprung und Ziel der Geschichte*, 1949, p.20; ET, 1953, p.21.

6. *Ibid.*, p. 15; ET, p. xiii.

7. *Op. cit.*, 1940; cited from the revised edition, *Christentum und Geschichtlichkeit*, 1951.

8. *Op. cit.*, pp. 8f.

9. *Ibid.*, pp. 18f.

10. *Ibid.*, p. 9 n.

11. *Ibid.*, p. 43.

12. *Ibid.*, p. 44.

13. *Ibid.*, p. 20.

14. *Ibid.*, p. 21.

15. *Ibid.*, p. 348.

16. First published in English in 1949; the German verison, *Weltgeschichte und Heilsgeschehen. Die theologischen Voraussetzungen der Geschichtsphilosophie*, appeared in 1953.

17. There are however no signs that Löwith was in any way influenced by British or American biblical scholarship.

18. *Op. cit.*, p. 189.

19. 'Both Heidegger and Bultmann insist that the "true" futurity of the human and divine *eschaton*, respectively, lies in the instant of our decision. They ignore the fact that neither death nor the Kingdom of God could ever provoke a decision, and even less a radical change in man's conduct and attitude, unless they were expected as real events in the future' (p.253 n. 21).

20. Like Löwith's book, Eric Voegelin's vast work *Order in History* (1956ff.) was written in America, but it is none the less stamped by German philosophy and theology. Voegelin traces the ways in which men have determined the order of their society in the course of history, by transforming and fixing the 'real' by means of symbolic forms. He presents a 'history of symbolization' (I, p.5) in which Christianity plays a decisive role. A whole volume is devoted to 'Israel and Revelation'. No special role is assigned to apocalyptic literature, though it is mentioned occasionally (I, p.454, for example).

21. One example may serve for many: N.Jankowski's 'Entlarvte Apo-kalypse' ('Apo-kalypse exposed'; what is meant are the aims of the APO - the 'ausserparlementarische Opposition' - the non-parliamentary opposition, or radical student group), in the weekly *Die Zeit*, 4 April 1969, p. 13.

22. *Technik und Wissenschaft als 'Ideologie'* (Edition Suhrkamp 287), 1968, pp. 65f.

23. *Op. cit.*, p. 28. Cf. the critique of U. Wilckens: 'Zur Eschatologie des Urchristentums' in *Beiträge zur Theorie des neuzeitlichen Christentums, Festschrift für W. Trillhaas*, ed. by H.J. Birkner and D. Rössler, 1968, pp. 127-42. Blumenberg rests his argument on the contrast (so much favoured by theologians) between eschatology and historical progress, and heightens the distinction into a crass contrast.

24. *Atheismus im Christentum*, 1968, pp. 98ff.

25. *Ibid.*, p. 23.

26. *Ibid.*, p. 22; cf. p. 63.

27. *Ibid.*, p 64.

28. *Ibid.*, p. 173.

29. *Ibid.*, p. 171.

30. *Ibid.*, p. 176.

31. *Europe: a Prophecy*, lines 198-200. But Bloch here uses a fantastically free German translation to make his point. 'Orc' becomes 'the Spirit of rebellion' and Enitharmon is translated as 'the Saviour'. The first two lines therefore become: 'The Spirit of rebellion shot down by the Saviour.'

INDEX OF NAMES

Käsemann, E., 14, 73, 75-85, 147
Kautzsch, E., 13, 50, 95, 132
Kierkegaard, S., 80
Kittel, R., 60
Klatt, W., 138
Klein, G., 147, 151f.
Koch, K., 137, 138, 139, 140, 150
Köhler, L., 38
König, F., 149
Kraft, H., 62, 133
Kuhn, K. G., 118
Kümmel, W. G., 63, 93, 133, 144, 146
Kutscher, E. Y., 133

Ladd, G. E., 142
Lagrange, M. J., 95
Lessing, G. E., 98
Lindblom, J., 137
Lohmeyer, E., 61f., 133, 150
Lohse, E., 132
Loisy, A., 150
Löwith, K., 118f., 154

McCown, C. C., 149
Manson, T. W., 142
Manson, W., 54f., 142
Marcuse, H., 131
Marxsen, W., 93
Ménard, J. E., 133
Meyer, E., 138
Moltmann, J., 106-9, 130, 152
Moore, G. F., 50, 86
Mundle, W., 143
Müntzer, T., 122
Murdock, W. R., 86, 90f., 135, 148, 150

Neuman, A., 133
Nissen, A., 86-8, 133, 137, 139, 148, 151
Noth, M., 39, 139

Oesterley, W. O. E. 134
Osten-Sacken, P. von der, 141
Otto, R., 136, 144

Pannenberg, W., 14, 75, 88, 90, 101-9, 127, 130, 137, 146, 149, 151f.
Pfeiffer, R. H., 140
Plöger, O., 21, 39-42, 45, 46, 49, 53, 109, 139

Porteous, N., 138

Rad, G. von, 42-7, 49, 52, 88, 102, 107, 133, 134, 136, 139, 140, 141, 151
Ratzinger, J., 110
Reicke, B., 93, 133
Renan, E., 121
Rendtorff, R., 137
Ringgren, H., 33, 139
Robinson, J. M., 145, 151
Rössler, D., 40-2, 45, 49, 53, 73f., 85, 87-90, 101-105, 139, 147, 148, 149, 154
Rowley, H. H., 38, 51-3, 68, 105, 134, 141
Russell, D. S., 22, 49, 52-4, 133, 134, 137, 142
Rylaarsdam, J. C., 141

Sabatier, P., 53
Sauter, G., 106, 108f., 132
Schmidt, J. M., 137, 138, 140
Schmidt, K. L., 146
Schmoldt, H., 136
Schnackenburg, R., 64
Schneemelcher, W., 132, 133, 137, 148
Schulz, S., 133
Schürer, E., 37, 95, 138
Schweitzer, A., 58f., 71, 100
Sellin, E., 47, 141
Simon, M., 96
Stauffer, E., 63, 144
Steck, O. H., 139, 140
Strack, W. L., 60, 86
Strobel, A., 85f.
Stuhlmacher, P., 85

Tedesche, S., 132
Tödt, H. E., 145
Trillhaas, W., 152
Trilling, W., 64

Vawter, B., 142
Vielhauer, P., 68, 84, 118, 132, 135, 136, 148
Violet, B., 133, 136
Voegelin, E., 154
Volz, P., 13, 38, 86

Weber, H. E., 150
Weiss, J., 57f.